Molo Mama Jenny Warmkelekile esikolweni Sethu

HELLO MRS JENNY
WELCOME TO OUR SCHOOL!

VOLUNTEERING IN A SOUTH AFRICAN TOWNSHIP

JENNY BAKER

Published in 2017 by Jenny Baker

© Copyright Jenny Baker

ISBN: 978-1-5272-1331-9

Book Design by Russell Holden

 Pixel Tweaks Publications
SELF-PUBLISHING MADE SIMPLE

www.pixeltweakspublications.com

Printed by Ingram

ACKNOWLEDGEMENTS

My thanks go to Steve and Kay for their wonderful *Ways with Words* writing and painting holidays.

To tutors Mark McCrum and Blake Morrison for helping me to turn one paragraph into a book.

To my friend, the writer Janet Denny, for her encouragement and support.

My teachers Zozo, Cynthia, Miss January, & Ludwe for welcoming me so warmly into their classrooms.

Last by no means least to my granddaughter Yasmin Azarya for helping me negotiate the pitfalls of modern technology.

I dedicate this book to the memory of Paul Miedema, a truly inspirational man, and to the children I met while teaching at Isaac Booi. They are the future of South Africa. They deserve a better world.

CONTENTS

CHAPTER ONE

"ABOUT THE POETRY," SAID ZOZO

"About the poetry, Jenny," said Zozo. "Please will you help me to teach it? I do not know how to teach the poetry."

It was the end of a lesson at Isaac Booi Primary School in Zwide, a township in the Eastern Cape, South Africa. Forty black children rushed past me, eager for short break.

"Goodbye, Mrs Jenny!"

"Thank you, Mrs Jenny."

"Thank you, teacher!"

In fact, Zozo was the teacher, I the volunteer. She was tall, statuesque, warm and loving. She turned and hugged me; it was only my fourth day at the school but already we were friends. "About the poetry," she repeated. "Please will you help me? I cannot teach the poetry." I did not know how to answer her question. How could I begin sharing poetry with a class of forty-two township children whose main language was Xhosa?

As I stood in that classroom my thoughts travelled back to the morning four months previously when the postman had pushed a brochure through my door. It was large and wrapped in film. I cursed silently. "What a waste of paper," I thought. It was from Saga and I did not even want to look at it; package holidays without my wonderful husband Bob were unthinkable.

Yet I hesitated before throwing it in the recycling bin. Maybe I would just glance at it. I was in the middle of lunch, my book was upstairs, I was too lazy to get it and I needed something to read. The brochure was heavy and as I put it down on the table it fell open. Instead of glossy pictures of exotic holiday destinations, I saw just five words:

VOLUNTEERING! IS IT FOR YOU?

I read on, the baked beans on my plate growing congealed and cold. It wouldn't hurt just to enquire, I told myself: the number was free, after all. I picked up the phone and dialled.

"Hello," I said hesitantly, "I want to ask about volunteering."

That was a decisive moment in my life.

***

For weeks before I was due to leave I was full of apprehension. It was January and on my last day in England the weather was icy, dangerously so; my steep drive was totally impassable. My diary was full of last minute appointments - hairdresser, doctor, chiropodist -and I was almost convinced that I should not be going. I was feeling desperate when the back doorbell rang. It was Miles, my gardener. He had been invaluable since Bob's death, helping me with so many small tasks. He stood there at the door, a cap on his head and his boots covered in ice. "Thought you might need some help," he said, "you'll not get down the drive in your car."

I was so relieved to see him.

"Oh please Miles, will you take me into Ambleside?"

He was delighted and I managed to do all my tasks, getting home just as a threatened snowstorm arrived. I still had many jobs to finish but I was exhausted and fell into bed, leaving the last of my packing till the morning.

What a morning! I woke at 6am and switched my radio on. Nothing happened. The house was in darkness. I stumbled to the window and pulled open the curtains but there were no lights to be seen. Everything was white. I finished packing by the light of a torch, I had managed to find one in a drawer. It was growing lighter. I could now see that snow, about three inches thick, was covering my bird table. In other places it had formed into huge drifts, and the road filled me with horror. How would a taxi possibly reach me? And what was I, a wrinkly grandmother, doing travelling thousands of miles to volunteer in a township school anyway?

The time passed as I fumbled around. I longed for a cup of tea. The taxi was due at 8.45am. I looked at my watch: it was already 8.40. I scanned the road anxiously but saw no cars. Picking up my mobile phone, I went out in the garden to try and get a signal. It was very beautiful but certainly not a day for travelling! As I was desperately trying to ring the number Saga had given me, I saw a man trudging up the steep steps through my garden. The snow was up to his knees.

"Are you ready?" he asked. "I only just managed to get here, your road is almost blocked. There are several abandoned cars. We'd better get going quickly."

I thanked him as he manoeuvred my large case through the garden, me following in my welly boots. The sandals that I had thought I would travel in had been hastily jammed into my rucksack.

I slipped and slithered down the path and climbed into the taxi, relief flooding through me. But what on earth could I do with my boots? I could not take them to South Africa. As the taxi rounded the corner I saw my lovely neighbours Davina and Colin standing in their garden waving at me. The taxi driver had stopped at their house to ask for directions. The snow was too deep to get out of the taxi again so I opened the door, took my boots off and threw them to Davina and Collin. I was on my way!

Hours later, as I was sitting in the departure lounge, a man came up to me smiling.

"You must be Jenny Baker? I noticed the Saga label on your hand luggage."

This was how I first met Andrew and his friend Irene. I learned that they too were volunteers with Saga. It was the start of our friendship.

We travelled through the night and the journey seemed interminable: I could not sleep and was filled with apprehension and excitement. Arriving in the morning in Johannesburg we had to collect our cases and book in again for the last part of the journey.

When we finally landed in Port Elizabeth the sun was out. I blinked as I walked out into the light: it was such a contrast to the wintry world I had left behind. As we travelled the short distance from the airport to the hotel I noticed that most of the expensive looking houses were surrounded by heavily spiked railings and locked gates. I was too tired to talk to the other volunteers and I was grateful when our minibus stopped outside the Humewood Hotel. It looked reassuringly familiar, I had often looked at photographs of it. The middle rounded portion with its blue and white façade somehow made me think of a giant birthday cake. Built in 1900 it was billed as the friendliest hotel in Port Elizabeth, offering a home away from home. We were welcomed warmly and taken to our rooms.

My bedroom looked friendly and comfortable; it was also hot and stuffy, the air conditioning had not been switched on. There was a public pool opposite - I could see it from my window – and it curved invitingly, the water as blue as the sky. If I hurried, I could have a late afternoon swim.

It was glorious in the water. I was the only person in that vast pool, I wanted to stay longer, wash away the stiffness of the journey, but the large clock warned me that it would soon be closing time. The building seemed deserted and I showered quickly, my feet echoing as I walked to the exit. I pushed the turnstile... it did not move. I pushed and pushed and pushed but still it did not move. I began to panic. I had only been in South Africa for three hours and already I was in a serious predicament! There was no alternative: I would have to try and crawl under the turnstile. No easy feat for a wrinkly lady who had been travelling for 27 hours.

I crouched down and my knees creaked. I pushed my towel and costume under the iron bars. That was the easy part! Then I tried to wriggle through. I was halfway when I heard footsteps. Slowly, trying to look dignified, I managed to extricate myself and stand up. In front of me was a very large black man, a huge bunch of keys dangling from his waist. He was smiling. I blushed. "The turnstile was locked," I blurted out. "I thought everyone had left."

He laughed, "I was just at the other end of the building locking up. I knew you were still here."

I apologised and suddenly the world became normal again. I was so relieved to have escaped, I did not realise until later that my exploits had been captured on a security camera! However, the story had a happy ending as for all the three months that I spent in Port Elizabeth I was given half-price entry to the pool.

I got back to the Humewood Hotel just in time to change for dinner and to meet my fellow volunteers. Irene and Andrew were the first to appear, they were warm and friendly. Stuart joined us next: I had noticed him at the airport. He walked with a stick and I learned that he had caught polio as a child. He had just retired but his wife was still working so had remained at home. Finally, Sue came down. She too had just retired, having been headmistress of a nursery school.

It was our first evening together but I was so tired my memories have blurred. What I do know is that after the meal I climbed quickly and thankfully into bed.

• CHAPTER TWO •

INDUCTION DAY

During my conversations with Saga I had learned that their volunteer programme in South Africa was run by a firm called Calabash. Intrigued, I had Googled it and what I read interested me:

"Calabash Tours will expose you to the real Port Elizabeth. You'll see the historic city itself, the townships and the memorials. You'll meet real people. Port Elizabeth's struggle against apartheid has left it with a fascinating past and present."

Calabash Tours and its founder Paul Meidema were the most important factors in my final decision to volunteer. People sometimes asked Paul and his wife, Thandi, whether township tours aren't perhaps a little voyeuristic. Paul's response, which I quote from Calabash's website, was heartfelt:

"Township people are delighted to see visitors. They feel happy, their histories and their lives are now receiving attention and also that these previously overlooked areas are now seen as tourism attractions in their own right!"

Calabash Tours was also a Fairtrade Tourism[1] certified company, and this too had been a factor in my decision. I had started the Windermere and Bowness Fairtrade Group and been its co-ordinator for nine years; I was also a member of the steering committee of the Cumbria Fairtrade Network, which represented 23 Fairtrade towns.[2]

---

1 Fairtrade Tourism SA, is a non-profit making organisation promoting best practice in responsible tourism.
2 I do advise my readers to learn more about Calabash Tours and the Calabash Trust by visiting their website: www.calabashtours.co.za

stood on a table and posters exalting high ideals lined the walls. The toilet was clean but there was no toilet paper.

Emerging, I returned to the staffroom and found the Principal waiting for me. Beside him stood a large, imposing lady, her face was stern. She shook my hand but did not smile. The Principal introduced us but I was so nervous that I hardly heard her surname. I didn't like to ask him to repeat it - it was unpronounceable anyway - but her first name was short and easy to remember: Sox!

We sat down at a table and Sox pulled out of her bag a crumpled sheet of A4 paper covered in minute writing. This, I learned, was an English test with an incredibly complicated mark scheme. "My class is 9A," said Sox, "there is no 9B or 9C."

"How many children are in your class," I enquired.

"About fifty," she replied, "they are aged between 14 and 19 years."

The huge difference in ages was hard for me to grasp; I also wondered what teenagers were doing in a "primary school". I later discovered that all children have to pass a test at the end of each year before they can move up to the next grade. Many children miss years of schooling: township life is hard and AIDs affects people in so many different ways.

I listened to Sox as she explained her scheme of work, but after about ten minutes she stood up suddenly. "Jenny, goodbye. I am going shopping."

The Principal had also vanished and so I sat in the staffroom alone feeling slightly foolish. My completed timetable didn't exist: I had only one lesson with Sox and that was not until period 6. However I hadn't come all the way to South Africa just to sit in a staffroom, hesitantly I got up and walked to the door.

Venturing out, I passed the children's vegetable garden, dried by the January sun. Piles of litter lay everywhere: the recycled rubbish bins were ineffectual, they had no lids and there was a strong wind blowing. I walked down corridors, passing classrooms, hearing children chanting and teachers shouting. In many of the classrooms, however, there appeared to be no teachers. It was pandemonium. Children were yelling, running, pushing each other and moving desks and tables.

Finally, I came to a huge room, the door of which was ajar. Inside the Principal was speaking to hundreds of parents, mostly women. There were babies and toddlers but none of them made a sound; all sat impassively on their mother's laps.

I crept in, watched and listened and learned. I had already discovered that all children in the school were members of the Xhosa tribe and that many words in their language were prefixed by a click. In all my weeks at the school I never fully mastered this vocal trick despite the efforts of the older children to teach me. We always collapsed into giggles. However, this was my first day and I was fascinated. The Principal was clearly an orator and I was intrigued by the way he alternated seamlessly between Xhosa and English. Except for the occasional murmurs of assent from the parents, the room was silent. The speeches went on and on, teachers rose and spoke in turn, parents nodded their approval. After what seemed like hours I retreated to the staffroom. Sox had not returned. A lady entered, welcomed me and shook my hand Xhosa-style, with a three-way hand-shake.

"My name is Agnes," she said, "but everyone calls me Boni."

She was small in stature but she spoke with passion about the problems of the school and the parents. I was already learning that South Africa breeds people who care strongly about their country. Boni told me that 50 per cent of children had lost their parents through AIDs; she herself had two children of her own but had adopted two orphaned children. Was she a teacher, I wondered? No. When she rose to leave, she said, "It has been a pleasure to meet you. I am the chairman of the governors: I will be on holiday from work for the next three weeks and spending most of my time here in school, so we will meet again. Thank you for volunteering."

I was amazed. Would a chairman of governors in the UK be prepared to give up their holidays to work in school?

As the weeks passed I admired Boni more and more: we shared the same ideals and became friends. I often told her that I thought she should become the next President of South Africa! On that first day, however, it was time to go to my first lesson: Class 9A with Sox. I made my way up the filthy staircase to her classroom at the end of the top corridor. There was no sign of her. The top half of the door was glazed and, as I looked through it, I froze in horror. Inside about 50 kids were engaged in what seemed like a gigantic furniture removal operation. Books littered the floor, broken windows banged in the wind and ancient posters hung forlornly on beige walls. There were clearly not enough tables for the number of children and some sat with planks of wood on their knees in place of desks. There was much shouting, pushing and shoving and the noise echoed through my head. For the third time that day I was alone, feeling foolish, but my inner voice challenged me once again. "You're here: go in."

Jenny with Boni
Chairman of the Governors

13

Somehow I managed to open the door.

A succession of "shushes" travelled through the class. "Silence!" shouted one boy – he was a young man, really - and finally it fell quiet. I took a deep breath.

"Hello. I am Mrs Jenny and I have come from England to teach you."

Just at that moment Sox walked in. I breathed a huge sigh of relief. What I didn't know then was that in the weeks to come I wouldn't always be granted a reprieve.

***

I had been in the school for not much more than a week when Sox disappeared again. Once more I was alone in front of the class. The usual chaos ensued as I stood watching, wondering what I should do. At that moment the Principal entered, looking flustered. "I am sorry Jenny, Sox is away," he said, "but you do not need to teach alone: you can sit in the staffroom if you want." With that, he abruptly left.

A few minutes later, two other teachers were at my side: Zozo and Cynthia. "You do not need to teach alone Jenny, it is not right," they repeated reassuringly.

The children were staring at me and it was strangely quiet.

"It is OK," I said, "I will try and teach them."

I knew that every volunteer had the right to refuse to be alone in the classroom but I could not let the children down. ('Children' is the wrong word: they were young people not unlike my eldest grandchildren. Several of the boys had moustaches.) I left the classroom and found the Principal.

"How long will Sox be away?" I asked.

"I am sorry Jenny; I do not know. But she has asked me to tell you that she would like the class to learn how to compose a letter."

I returned to the classroom and it was only when I stood in front of the class that I fully realised what I was taking on. In my absence the noise had reached a crescendo: how could I possibly speak over it? I looked around for a bell or even a whistle but there was nothing. Suddenly the very tall boy who had saved me before stood up.

"Be quiet! Mrs Jenny wants to speak," he shouted in his deep voice.

I took a deep breath.

"Hello everyone, I am afraid your teacher is away. As you know I don't speak Xhosa, so please will you help me?"

The room was quiet. Everyone looked at me attentively and from that moment on I never had a problem - although I was always grateful when one of the oldest boys shouted for quiet at the beginning of the lesson.

Two-and-a-half weeks passed before Sox returned and in that time I got to know the class well. I told them about my teenage grandchildren and they in turn told me about their lives. I was struck by their maturity as we discussed the problems of growing up. We became friends and after many of the lessons I was actually clapped or cheered.

When Sox finally returned she gave me no explanation for her absence, and we taught for a further three days together. On the last day, Sox was very excited. "Jenny I am going to have a new kitchen! The kitchen man will come and give me a quotation."

I thought nothing more of our conversation until I had to go to the loo. On my way down the ever-dirty staircase I passed a swarthy man with a pad of paper in his hands. Sox greeted me excitedly when I got back to the classroom and waved a sheet of paper. "Jenny, the kitchen man has been, I will get my kitchen! It is a good quote!"

Happily, she showed me the plans. I was incredulous. How different this school was to the large comprehensive where I had taught in England.

On my second visit to Isaac Booi Sox greeted me with a huge hug. She was smiling broadly. "I have you in my bedroom Jenny, I have you in my bedroom," she cried. I was totally puzzled until she explained, "I have the photo of you and me in my bedroom."

When I returned to the school for the third time there was no sign of Sox. "She has left the school," Zozo told me, "she has just got married and she is very happy."

CHAPTER FOUR

"GOOD MORNING, MRS CYNTHIA CADELA, GOOD MORNING, MRS JENNY BAKER!"

My first week at Isaac Booi was one of perpetual confusion: I was constantly unsure of where I should be and what I should be doing.

Ludwe, the teacher responsible for volunteers, tried to help me but as he himself said, "Jenny, I am rushing around like a headless chicken." He seemed almost as confused as I was. However, I did at least get to know the other teachers, Cynthia and Zozo. Together with Sox and Ludwe we sat round a small table and I looked on perplexed while the others passed round minute slips of paper and talked earnestly about what "Jenny" should be doing. It seemed incredibly complicated and I became irritated by the constant confusion. In fact, it was not until the following Monday, five days after I had arrived in the school,

Jenny with Mrs Cynthia Cadela

17

that I got a timetable and even then I was still confused: it did not align with the times of lessons. I asked Cynthia about it.

"Oh Jenny," she replied. "It is 2013 but you have a 2012 timetable!"

I was lost for words.

In the three months I spent volunteering I never really got to grips with the timetable. It often changed and there were two alternative timetables with shortened periods used on special occasions such as sports day. In addition, the children all ate at different times: the four mothers who cooked meals in a small container on the premises could not cope with serving more than one class at a sitting. Consequently, I might be teaching one moment and the next watching as the children disappeared to eat having received no warning at all.

I was teaching several different classes – 9A, 8A, 8B, 7A and 7B. The classes were as confusing as the timetables. 9A was the top class in the school in 2013 and all contained a range of ages: even in 7A and 7B there were boys with moustaches.

I was largely teaching English, oral and written, with Zozo and Cynthia, although I learned that I would also be helping Patrick the Principal with "life skills". I quickly started team-teaching with Zozo and Cynthia and we became firm friends. I don't know when Cynthia and I started greeting each other as "Mrs Jenny Baker" and "Mrs Cynthia Cadela", but even today we often start emails this way.

Zozo and Cynthia were caring teachers and I was lucky to meet both their families on my second visit. Cynthia, a single mother, lived with her two teenage sons, who were both well-mannered and kind, and her cousin, who had a baby girl. Zozo was married and when we first met her eldest son was 16, her twin boys 13 and her little girl three. They were lovely children, full of fun and laughter, and her eldest son was very handsome. "Show Jenny your stomach," said Zozo when she introduced me to him. It was taut: his muscles rippled. Zozo loved clothes, every day she dressed in new outfits. Sometimes her hair was piled regally on the top of her head, other times it would be braided. She reminded me of an exotic bird.

In 2014 I invited her to come with her family to the Humewood Hotel. We all went swimming together. Afterwards we had lunch, I ordered plates of sandwiches and bowls of chips. I reflected that in the apartheid years it would have been impossible for a white, English grandmother to sit with a black family. We laughed and joked and I ordered more and more chips. At the end of lunch Zozo whispered in my ear, "thank you Jenny, now I want to take you for a special treat. We will go to Green Acres shopping centre. It is a great place. You will love it."

With Zozo and her family at the Humewood Hotel

I will never forget my first lesson with Zozo. It was English comprehension and there was a lot of opportunity for oral work. One boy in particular caught my attention: he was clearly much older than the rest of his classmates. His hand was always up and he answered eagerly with a grave expression on his face. Finally, the class settled down to write and I noticed that his work was very poor. After the lesson I sat down quietly beside him.

"You answered very well," I said.

His face lit up.

"I like school," he said. "I want to do well. I love football but I am not going to play so much, I need to learn."

As we talked on he told me that both his parents had died and so he had gone to live with his stepmother. She was very cruel, making him work all the time. He had not been allowed to go to school and had hated his life. "Now my elder brother is looking after me, I want to catch up with my school work. I go into the neighbour's house and borrow a book to help me with my spelling."

I had noticed a bookshop near the hotel and that afternoon I went to buy a small dictionary. I did not want to single my pupil out, so I asked Zozo for her help.

"Will you give this to Siphosuthanus?"

What an amazing name that boy had! And what an impression he made on me. I can still remember what he told me that day: "My dream is to build a school for the community. It will be founded by me, it will be very inclusive, black and white children will learn together, it will be free."

I taught him often during the next four weeks and he was always keen to answer my questions, but clearly found written work hard. I worried about him.

On my last day, he found me in the corridor and whispered in my ear.

"Thank you Mrs Jenny, I use the book always, I will try very hard."

I do not know what happened to him: when I found myself back at Isaac Booi the next year, he had moved to High School.

***

It was on my fourth day that Zozo asked me about poetry.

"Please Jenny, will you show me how to teach the poetry?"

I had felt very inadequate.

"I'll try," I replied. "Have you any poetry books?"

We went to look in her cupboard and piles of books fell out everywhere as she retrieved a small, tattered beige booklet. It smelt of the 1950's; it was torn, musty and full of rhymes. I muttered my thanks but secretly resolved to put it in the rubbish bin in my hotel room.

Zozo did not mention poetry again that day and I found myself hoping that this was a reprieve: maybe I would not have to teach it after all! However, when I entered her classroom the next day there it was a poem entitled "The Flamingo" on the blackboard. It was well written, simple yet complex, full of metaphors and similes.

"I found it in a magazine," said Zozo. She read it to the class as they listened intently, then I read it again. Her crimson jacket evoked the bright colour of the bird, a picture of Lake Windermere which I had brought with me showed reflections in the water. We created word pictures. Finally, I asked the children to close their eyes as I read "The Flamingo" again. They sat very still. When it was finished they remained silent for a moment and then started to clap and cheer.

Days later, and in broken English, they were hesitantly starting to write their own poems: "elephants plodding," "lions prowling", "leopards sleeping in the sun". How proud they were.

On my last morning I went into school carrying a large hardback book. It was full of pictures of wild South African animals: a present to the children to remind them of the poems they had written.

"You must present it to them, Jenny," said Zozo and she called a boy and a girl to the front of the classroom to receive the gift. The kids were thrilled.

"I will look after it, Jenny, we will use it and think about you," promised Zozo.

She kept her promise and a year later she told me that she was still sharing it with the children. "Some kids even come up to school in long break to look at it Jenny, they love it."

I still remember the last email she wrote to me about poetry:

Dear Jenny,

I love and miss you very much. About the poetry, now I can teach it. The children love it and I love it too.

Thank you, Zozo.

• CHAPTER FIVE •

HAPPY SAD SCHOOL

South Africa and Isaac Booi school had really got under my skin and by August 2013 I had already decided that I would return the following January. As it happens I also returned in 2015 and even now, after three visits, I find South Africa hard to write about in a logical way. It is so full of contrasts and contradictions and when I close my eyes at night many impressions, both good and bad, flash in front of me.

Before going to South Africa in 2013 I had read a book by Mark McCrum entitled *Happy Sad Land*. It was an account of the author's return to that country in 1992. He had previously visited during the apartheid years and wanted to record his impressions of a changed country and the thoughts of African people, from slum dwellers to Chief Mango-suthu Buthelezi, on the eve of the transition to majority rule.

Although my first visit was 21 years after Mark's book had been published, I found the country still happy, still sad. My impression of Isaac Booi was of a school full of laughter, hugs, songs and smiles. I remember one Valentine's Day in particular: the hundreds of children all dressed in red and white, eating hot dogs lovingly prepared by their teachers and dancing for hours. Majorettes marched up and down, resplendent in their red and white uniforms, and the choir sang proudly, all eyes on Miss January, their skilful conductor.

But the sadness, although more difficult to spot, was certainly there. I could see it in the parents who waited anxiously outside the Principal's door. I could hear it when teachers talked of losing their jobs, fearful of being moved with no notice. Children were scared of some of the teachers and a hush would settle over them when a male member of staff walked past, swinging a stick or carrying a sawn off piece of hosepipe. I shuddered when I heard of a boy being raped in the toilet.

The classrooms were sad places, hot and dusty. In many of them the windows were impossible to open or broken: great shards of glass like pointed daggers hung down and I feared for the safety of the children. Piles of broken furniture were stacked on the flat roof of the school and although no one mended it, throwing it away was forbidden. Often there were not enough chairs for all the children and many were unsafe: huge boys sat on seats designed for the reception class.

Theft was a common problem and everything had to be locked up. Twice I returned to the school after a weekend away only to find that the canteen had been burgled. In consequence, teachers guarded their cupboards and often kept books that were useless.

The school building itself was filthy. The sole caretaker, a tiny, wiry man, tried hard but his task was impossible. Many of the girls had no sanitary towels. They told me about the ghastly toilets." Cynthia confided that she sometimes stayed after school to clean the boy's toilets.

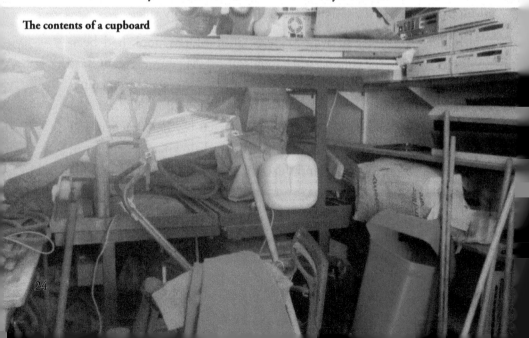

The contents of a cupboard

Children, and some parents of reception class children, attempted to clean the school themselves. One afternoon I saw a small boy trying to sweep rubbish onto a flimsy piece of paper.

"We teach our kids to be resourceful," Cynthia said when I told her what I had seen.

Then next morning I brought a strong metal dustpan with me to school, horrifying Cynthia. "It is too good Jenny; it will get stolen. We must lock it in the staffroom." Sadly, I expect it probably lies there still, too good to be used.

There were rubbish bins around the school and the children were encouraged to use them. They were made from recycled food cans, had no lids and as Port Elizabeth is a notoriously windy city the rubbish blew out of them and congregated in corners or on the stairs. On my second visit Christine, a fellow volunteer, and I bought large, strong bins with lids. The caretaker painted "ISAAC BOOI" on them in white paint and chained them to posts, but the litter seemed just as bad when I returned in 2015 and many of the bin lids were missing.

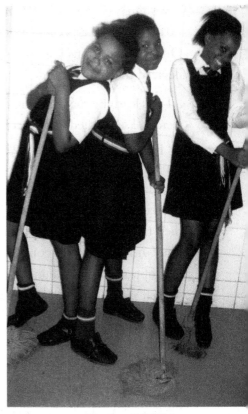

Resourceful Kids!

On so many occasions I grew angry with the corrupt government. I considered it was letting down the kids who were so eager to learn. And although I became very fond of the teachers, particularly the ones I taught with, they also angered me sometimes. There were countless times when lengthy staff meetings were held in school time and the children were left unattended. Teachers would arrive late and would often use their mobile phones during lessons.

We rarely had a week when the school didn't close early. Power cuts, (load shedding) especially in my last year, were an almost daily occurance On other occasions lessons would end at noon because the Government decreed that staff should count the furniture.

I was learning that, although apartheid had ended, the township schools were still segregated: not by colour, but by money and geography, blighted by poor buildings and a shortage of teachers. There was no money for supply teachers and as many as four classes could be left unattended at any one time. I marvelled that only rarely did a child get injured. One day I paused outside a class and saw all the children standing smartly, reciting their tables. There was no adult in sight. "Where is your teacher?" I asked. They did not know. I could not help but contrast their behaviour with that of pupils in an English primary school. Would our children behave so well if left unattended? I praised the class and they beamed at me. I took a photo and left. As I walked down the corridor I could hear them still chanting.

Usually, however, the absence of teachers meant that the school was never quiet. I found trying to teach above the noise very difficult, sometimes impossible. In class many of the children were shy, mumbling the answers to questions, and I found myself darting around the classroom in order to hear each individual. "Mrs Jenny is getting old," I would say bending down beside them, "please speak loudly."

Rote learning predominated at Isaac Booi, with teachers standing at the blackboard and shouting instructions. The kids chanted in unison but I often felt that they had little real understanding. Comprehension exercises were way above their abilities. They pretended that they understood but often the vocabulary used would be difficult even for English pupils of a similar age. However, they responded well in group situations and after the initial chaos took part in mature discussions – I often used drama in my lessons and they loved it.

On my third visit to Isaac Booi a group of parents asked to see me. I already knew that, four weeks into the start of the New Year, the school was still two teachers short, one of them in the Reception class. A parent was voluntarily trying to help.

When I returned home after my first visit to Isaac Booi I learned that members of staff had gone on strike for a month to protest against the shortage of teachers in the school.

"Jenny, please can you help us? Our children have no teacher, we are desperate," one parent begged. She had tears in her eyes. "The Principal goes to the department every day but still we wait. Now a deputation of parents will visit the department: please will you come with us?"

"Yes, Jenny, please come with us," they implored. It was Thursday; I had to tell them that Friday would be my last day at the school. I felt terrible.

On my last visit to Isaac Booi a high school teacher specialising in the education of 18 year olds was sent to teach the Reception class. It seemed mad. She was sent away and the post remained vacant.

In 2013 I entered the school one day and found many of the teachers in tears. One member of staff who had been at the school for 12 years had been told that she would have to relocate to another school 150 miles away. She had just four days' notice. She was a much-loved and excellent teacher and a leaving party was hastily convened. There were many emotional speeches but no one could do anything about it.

Even the cooks who worked tirelessly in their small tin hut to cook for hundreds of children came to see me to ask for assistance. "Jenny, our contract runs out in March, please can you help us find a job?"

Once again I felt helpless. Those ladies worked so hard in their small tin kitchen. They cooked throughout the day and the kids ate at different times, sitting or standing outside. The meals looked nourishing and the cooks always had smiles on their faces.

Rubbish and cardboard were piled in a huge heap on the field, one day I smelt smoke and saw enormous flames leaping up. I investigated and was horrified to see a group of unattended children fanning the fire.

Another time, I saw a 17-year-old girl standing outside the Principal's office. She looked surly and rebellious - she reminded me of some of the girls I had taught. Eventually she was joined by another woman. They looked very alike so I guessed that this was her mother. Every time I walked through the school I saw them both still standing, waiting. The girl's face was tearstained. I asked Zozo what was the matter. "The girl is 18, Jenny: really she should be at high school. She got teased by some boys because she was wearing primary school uniform. Now she refuses to wear uniform so she cannot come to school."

I thought of my own granddaughters and I could not help but sympathise with the girl.

Sometimes the pace of life at Isaac Booi was maddeningly slow. I was always keen to get on and it was very frustrating. Zozo often accused me of being a workaholic. Many teachers seemed to spend time sitting idly in the staffroom and were often late to lessons. In contrast I learned that they gave up their time to supervise after-school activities. Zozo taught squash, Cynthia coached a highly successful netball team, Ludwe took his rugby squad to England and Miss J lead the wonderful school choir. But I told myself not to judge: I was a guest in the school, after all. I also knew that teachers such as Zozo and Cynthia really cared for their pupils. I had to remind myself that I had no personal experience of township life and could not even begin to imagine the many difficulties that the teachers at its schools faced.

CHAPTER SIX

ASSEMBLIES AND PARENTS' MEETINGS

Assemblies were a vital part of the school day. Even now I can shut my eyes and see the children filing onto the outdoor space in between the two blocks of classrooms. There was no indoor hall: when a large indoor space was needed two classrooms could be made into one but it was not big enough to hold all the school.

The start of assembly was often chaotic. Kids would rush in from all directions, pushing, shoving and kicking. Then one child would start to sing and others would join in until the whole school was united effortlessly in harmony. They would pray earnestly, hands clasped, eyes shut tight. They looked so smart, not least because teachers patrolled the lines, urging the children to stand straight and pay attention. I was always moved as behind the smart uniforms and the smiling faces some squinted in the sun and others yawned. How far had they walked and what horrors had they seen? I wondered.

Every morning about six hundred children would gather. Teachers were often late, the male members of staff always dressed in smart suits and matching ties, their shoes shone. Many of the female teachers wore brightly coloured dresses. The school had a record of sporting success, rugby and netball were hugely important. In assembly many awards were given out, sporting heroes were clapped and cheered loudly.

Some mornings a tiny man would appear speaking in Xhosa. I learned that he was a preacher, paid to come and take assembly.

Some words I could recognise. He would urge everyone to repent, flinging his arms wide in the manner of an American TV evangelist. "Hallelujah!" he would shout and the children would shout "Hallelujah!" in unison. One morning he finished his exaltations in English.

"You will be saved by the blood of the Lord!" he cried.

I reflected on how easy it would be to indoctrinate children, so was pleased to see that some were restless, slyly pushing each other.

The notices seemed interminable: first the Principal, then many of the other teachers, spoke. I tried to understand. One morning the Principal shouted angrily at some children. Two boys and two girls were brought to the front in tears. The other children were laughing and jeering.

"What is happening?" I whispered to Zozo.

"They have been kissing in the toilets. It is disgusting, they are only eight years old."

I felt distinctly uncomfortable as the jeering grew louder and the four children cried.

***

Parents' meetings were frequent at the start of term. One day I was in the staffroom early in the morning as the next meeting, due to start at 10am, was being planned. The discussion was in Xhosa so I sat there daydreaming until I heard one word constantly repeated: "Jenny, Jenny, Jenny."

Everyone looked at me.

"What are they talking about?" I quietly asked Cynthia.

"You are to speak at the parents' meeting, Jenny," she replied. "You must tell the parents that we need their help."

"Oh!" was all I could say.

As I arrived at the meeting later that day I wondered if Cynthia had been joking. Hundreds of parents were filing in, some squatting on little chairs, others queuing at the door. Boni was sitting at a large table flanked by two teachers and, seeing me, she beckoned and patted the empty seat beside her. I sat down and looked around. I was the only white person in the room. "If only Bob could see me now," I thought to myself.

The speeches started, meaningless to me. Small babies strapped to their mothers lay quiet or sleeping while toddlers sat silent, their eyes wide. Once again I heard my name and, thinking this was my cue to speak, I half rose.

"Not yet, Jenny," whispered Boni.

The voices rose and fell. Sometimes a parent would shout out a phrase and others would cry out in agreement. Everyone looked solemn. Again I heard my name and Boni gestured that I should stand up. "You speak now," she said.

The room was quiet. I took a deep breath.

"Moloweni, everyone. I am pleased to be here. This is my third visit to Isaac Booi. I love the school, the teachers and your kids."

I paused and looked around.

"I too am a parent; I am also a grandmother. I know you love and care for your children as I do mine and that you want the best for them."

Many parents cried out, "Yes, we do love our kids!"

There was a pause.

"Will you help me, then?" I asked. "Will you make this school a better place for your children? There is so little money, the school is dirty, will you help?"

Mothers were nodding in agreement and one shouted out, "Yes, Jenny, I will help."

Finally, everyone was shouting excitedly: "Yes, we will help, tell us what we can do!"

"Thank you," I said. "We will have a meeting on Monday after school. Please write your name down if you would like to come."

By the time they had finished there were 21 names on the list. All were women.

"Bring some men," I said, at which they laughed and shrugged. Secretly I wondered if anyone would actually come.

Parents Meeting

The parents' meeting lasted all morning, but finally it finished. I expected that the normal timetable would resume in the afternoon so ate lunch quickly and prepared to go to my lessons. But when I got to the classroom there were no children. Instead, the kids were running and jumping in the corridors and stairways; others were swinging from the palm tree outside. I could not see any teachers until I met Miss January in the corridor.

"What is happening, Thumé? Everyone seems to have gone crazy."

"I do not know," she replied, "but I am going to have a choir practice."

When I met the Principal, I repeated the same question.

"What is happening Patrick?"

"I do not know Jenny, it is chaotic!" he said, shaking his head sadly as he retreated to his office. I could not see any other teachers.

I felt so sad: the children's education was disrupted like this on a daily basis. Often the school had to be shut because of a shortage of power in the province and the constant power-cuts caused huge difficulties.

When Monday came there was no power-cut, but I still wondered if any parents would come to the meeting. I confessed my doubts to Cynthia.

"Yes, Jenny, they will come. You will see they will come. We must plan the meeting: we must have refreshments; we must make them welcome."

At 3.30pm mothers were gathering outside the staff room. I invited them in, welcomed them and asked them to sit down. I counted 16, and there was also a representative of the Calabash Trust, Julie. I was glad of her support. Only one man was in attendance and he looked rather embarrassed.

Cynthia welcomed the parents and asked for their cooperation. Then I spoke about the Calabash Trust and introduced Julie. She explained that in many schools parents helped by assisting teachers, decorating, cleaning and so on. We divided into groups, each with a spokesperson.

One of the mothers.

All the mothers were keen to contribute and it seemed that there was a consensus: they would help with the cleaning when school ended on Friday. Once again I was doubtful as to whether they would keep to their word, but when Friday came the parent volunteers were there at 2.30pm, eager to begin. They worked hard but there was a lack of buckets and mops so that evening I went out and bought 12 brightly coloured buckets and 12 mops. The following Monday I arrived with my buckets and mops which the children seized from me instantly. They made a colourful parade, twirling the mops and dancing, and I took photos of them and made them into thank you cards for the mothers who had helped.

Sadly I never saw that one father again.

CHAPTER SEVEN

THE STAFFROOM & PAINTING THE WALLS

In 2013 I volunteered with Christine, she was a lovely, caring grand-mother. Towards the end of our last week we purchased enough paint to decorate the walls of four classrooms. The Principal drove us to the paint shop. I was excited, envisaging wonderful bright colours. We walked along the rows and rows of paint in the superstore. It was almost like being in B&Q or Do It All. Almost, but not quite. We searched and searched for those bright colours but could only find large quantities of paint in peach or white. We had to settle for peach.

"Who will decorate the walls?" I asked the Principal as we drove back to the school.

"The parents will help," he answered vaguely.

Our trip to the store was on a Friday and when we returned to the school on Monday morning I was met by Boni, the chairman of the governors.

"It is finished," she exclaimed, "we have painted four classrooms, the children helped me. I'm so tired, we started at eight o'clock and finished at six. The ladies came into the school to cook for us. Come and look Jenny."

I was astounded. I went with her to the first classroom. Every wall was painted, we walked on looking at all four rooms.

"Boni, you are amazing," I said. "Can you get all the kids together who helped you?"

Boni and her amazing team of volunteer painters

She did and at assembly that morning they stood proudly in front of the whole school while everyone clapped and cheered. I knew that my first impression of Boni had been right. She is an amazing woman.

During lunchtime the women teachers all came to the staffroom. There was much laughing, joking, hugging and singing. The male members of staff usually sat outside under the willow tree during Long Break. I rarely got a chance to talk to them. Children constantly knocked on the door, arriving with piles of books. Girls washed up the teacher's cups & brushed the floor. Men, it was always men, arrived bearing piles of brightly coloured materials for sale & the female members of staff would rummage enthusiastically through them often buying large quantities for new dresses.

On my third visit to the school I was the only white person.

"Speak English for me," I would laughingly tell them. Colour ceased to exist for me & I hope, for them. I was just Jenny or *JennyGran*, another member of staff.

Often there were lengthy Trade Union meetings. Teachers seemed to be paid very little and they needed to secure their rights. Everyone spoke passionately in Xhosa, occasionally some English words crept in. Although I could not speak the language it was obvious that the Unions were powerful.

CHAPTER EIGHT

THE FIRST LEAVING CEREMONY

During my first four weeks at Isaac Booi I often heard teachers talking about the leaving ceremony. As my final day grew nearer I became more curious. "What actually happens at the leaving ceremony?" I asked Zozo.

"It is a secret Jenny, I cannot tell you," she replied with a laugh. Then she gave me a warning: "You will need a large box of tissues."

The last morning came and I entered the staffroom feeling sad and a little apprehensive. The four weeks had passed so quickly. Cynthia was the first teacher I met and I gasped when I saw her in a beautiful lime green dress. "Wow! Cynthia, you look amazing," I said.

"This is traditional Xhosa, Jenny: I am wearing it for you because it is your last day. Look, the others will also wear their best clothes."

She was right: the teachers were transformed, each one seemed more resplendent than the last. I was glad that I had worn a brightly patterned skirt. Many of the women had painted traditional patterns on their faces and even the men had abandoned shirts and ties for traditional dress.

I went to my first lesson knowing that it would be the last that I would share with Zozo, but when I got to the classroom she was not there. I was concerned. I knew that she had been unwell for several days with a cyst on her face and I could tell that it was troubling her. The children came in and I realised that I would have to start the lesson alone. I was relieved when she walked in about 10 minutes later.

"Sorry Jenny, I am not feeling very well," she said and hugged me tightly. She looked incredible in a white dress with a separate shawl, its black beads intricately woven in a triangular pattern round her neck and over her shoulders. Huge silver earrings hung from her ears and a white cap adorned with coloured beads sat on her head. "I have painted my face for you, Jenny. Come, we must have our photo taken together."

She put her arm around me and we smiled at the camera. I often look at that picture and remember that day. The lesson finished and Zozo thrust a large brown envelope into my hand. "This is for you, Jenny," she said and with that she hurried off. The children had all left and I was alone in the classroom. I sat down and opened the letter. What I read brought tears to my eyes.

Jenny with Zozo

My dear Jenny

It is very sad when the one you love is
is leaving. I am deeply worried. I've learnt
a lot from you, your kindness, caring, sharing
especially sharing the knowledge you have, I will
miss your beautiful smile. About the poem; since I
told you it was difficult to teach, I can teach
it now with confidence! And you know what?
the kids did understand what you taught
them I'm happy and they are happy too!!
Thanks for the the things you've done for the
kids, parents and for the school too!!

I'm sorry Jenny I won't be able to attend
your farewell because at 11h00 I will be on
my way to theatre in order to be operated
the cyst near my ear. I endured the pains
for a week now because I didn't want to
be absent whilest you still here at school now
its too much to me I'm feeling the pains right
now but you won't see that.

  God bless you and your family!"
I love you to bits Jenny ♡

The letter written by Zozo

I could not believe that Zozo had been hiding her pain from me. I felt so worried about her. I rushed to the staffroom but sadly she had already gone.

Somehow I got through the rest of the morning. I was eating my lunch in the staffroom when the reception teacher walked in. "Jenny, come to my classroom. The children want to see you. They have a surprise for you."

When I entered the room I saw all the little ones lined up, their faces serious, their eyes huge.

"Now you are going to sing for Mrs Jenny," their teacher said.

They stood up. "In a cottage in a wood," they chorused, miming the actions to the song that I had taught them earlier and about which I write in chapter nine. I felt in my pocket for the tissues and quickly got out my iPad to take a picture: I wanted to capture a very special moment.

When I returned to the staffroom, it was transformed. The tables were covered in white cloths and adorned with vases of plastic flowers and there were programmes in front of every chair. Nearly all the teachers were already there.

After a leaving Ceremony

Cynthia grabbed my arm and propelled me to a seat in the middle of a large table. Boni, the chairman of the governors, was sitting on my right and another governor was on my left. Glancing at the programme I realised that this was going to be a long ceremony: prayers followed by speeches from Boni, the Principal and Cynthia, more prayers, entertainment by the students, then more prayers and finally a speech by Paul Miedema.

I sat down and the singing started, louder and more fervent than I had ever heard it before. I was glad of the box of tissues before me. The teachers' voices soared high, perfectly blending, they swayed rhythmically and clapped as they sang.

My fellow volunteer Sue was sharing the ceremony with me and her class marched in beaming proudly, singing "If you're happy and you know it". I looked across at Sue. Her eyes were filled with tears and she was biting her lip.

Then "my kids" walked in to form a choir from some of the older classes I had taught. I reached again for my iPad: I wanted to capture the moment. They stood in front of me singing and moving enthusiastically. As their voices rose to a crescendo one girl started keening[3]; others joined in and their voices got louder and louder.

Finally, the children marched out and Boni stood up and turned to me. I have forgotten most of the speech she made, but one phrase stays in my mind: "You are saving South Africa, Jenny and Sue."

Of course we weren't: I felt uncomfortable at such lavish praise. I was sure I had learned as much from the staff, pupils and parents at Isaac Booi as they had learned from me. But I smiled at Boni.

The speeches went on and on and on. I glanced at my watch: I wasn't bored, but I was embarrassed by the extravagant praise. I thought of Zozo and wished she were there too.

---

3 Making a wailing sound.

After the ceremony

Eventually Class 9 walked in, many of them seeming like adults. I looked at them and thought of the special bond we had formed when I had been left with them on my own. One girl sang solo and as her voice grew louder others joined in. When the singing finished another of the girls stepped forward and spoke. I still treasure her words although I don't think that I deserve them. I did so little and gained so much.

Then Paul stood up to make his speech. I had intended to record it on my iPad but by this time I was so full of emotion I touched the screen in the wrong place. Some of the teachers shouted, "Speech Jenny! You speak now!" my knees were trembling. Gingerly, I stood up and thanked them. Then the staff rose to their feet, singing and dancing. Cynthia grabbed my hands and together we went around the staffroom, laughing and clapping, as the ceremony came to an end.

I will never forget it!

DEAR mrs Jenny Baker.

As we Grade 9 pupils we want to take this time to thank you for being with us, these few f weeks you were with us. We also want to thank you for all the things you did for us, We wish you a safe Journey on your way back to ENGLAND, we'd also like to thank you for the time you have been with us in South Africa and in our school. It was realy good to be with you, we wish we could extend the time, but unfortunate we can't. After you have left you will open a woidest space in he our hearts, and we will miss you big time. We realy enjoyed spending time with each of you, you're a teacher, parent. told us what to do, when to do it. we appriciate all the things you tought us we will never forget them and you. The space that will remain will be treasured forever, until we meet again. You're so kind to us and a very loving person, may God double your blessings even more, you're soo friendly kind and you are a child would want in a parent. May God bless your trip, arrive home safely so that see all of you again. And also thanks for the words of wisdom. We realy appriciate your time and everything you did for us. We love you more than words can express. please send our kind regards to the people in England You'll be treasured for ever ms Jenny baker.

The speech given by a member of class 9

• CHAPTER NINE •

MORE MEMORIES

One day I was in the staffroom preparing for my first lesson when Cynthia walked in. "You are coming to the athletics meeting Jenny," she said. "Quickly get ready."

I was confused - I had expected to be teaching. I had no sunhat, no sunglasses, no water and it was very hot.

"Hurry, come Jenny! We must go," Cynthia urged me.

I walked to Cynthia's car where there were more teachers waiting. We set off but after a few minutes we pulled up outside a supermarket and all got out.

There was much deliberation and endless consultation about what drinks should be bought for the children. Cynthia got some money out of an envelope but 10 minutes passed and they were still talking.

"What is happening?" I asked Cynthia. That same question always seemed to be on my lips.

"Jenny, we have to buy some drinks for the kids but we do not have enough money."

I offered to give her some but she declined and so we piled back into the car and still the discussion continued. I was puzzled and confused. Why go to a supermarket if you do not have enough money?

We drove for some time, everyone chatting animatedly, then we arrived at another supermarket. Cynthia went in but came out almost immediately. "The supermarket is not the right one," she announced and drove off again.

"The athletics meeting will be over before we get there," I thought to myself. Finally, however, we arrived - although we still had not got any drinks. The stadium was very big and there were hordes of kids shouting and cheering. I was given a large sunhat and a seat but no one mentioned anything about refreshments. "This is Africa," I thought.

I watched the kids running and jumping with natural grace and skill. They gave their all, some collapsing or crying at the end and others actually being physically sick.

My attention was suddenly claimed by a very large man and an equally large woman who were attempting to put up a gazebo. They appeared to be having great difficulty. Finally, it was erected and they carried it to where some officials were sitting. Carefully the couple placed it over them, but to my amazement they did not secure it to the ground. Within seconds it blew away. The man and woman attempted to run after it but in the end they gave up and it lay forlornly on the ground.

Promptly at noon the Principal arrived to take me back in time for the Calabash bus. I suspected that Cynthia had asked him to be punctual. We talked as he drove and he told me was nearing retirement. I sensed that he was looking forward to it. He also told me that in South Africa a Principal is not allowed to choose his own teachers. He looked tired and defeated and I thought how dealing constantly with corruption and bureaucracy must be so frustrating.

***

My timetable had several free lessons on it, time that I would usually spend preparing. But often I walked around the school just looking, listening and learning. The building was in a terrible state. In some of the classrooms the ceilings were badly damaged: there were great holes where flimsy tiles had fallen down. Many of the floor tiles were also missing. I had tried in vain to get drawing pins into the hard walls - blue-tac just peeled off.

Sometimes I would venture into classrooms other than my own. In one I found Maureen, a small, fierce, almost boyish teacher who often wore a peaked cap. She taught Grade 5 and one day I tentatively opened her classroom door.

"Come in, Jenny!" she shouted. "You teach!"

The children were young and spoke hardly any English but everyone was looking at me expectantly.

"You teach, Jenny!" Maureen repeated.

What could I do?

I reached into my bag and pulled out a laminated, enlarged photo of my tiny spaniel, Becky. Immediately the children were attentive and with simple gestures I tried to describe her.

"Becky shakes a paw," I said, miming. "Becky barks, Becky goes for a walk." Suddenly I became aware that Maureen had become a dog! She sat, she begged, she pretended to lift a paw, to bark and to wag her tail. Gradually she drew me in, pretending to ask to be taken for a walk. Soon she was on all fours, her bottom wriggling from side to side. With the aid of a belt I led her round the classroom: anyone looking in would have wondered what on earth we were doing. The children were all laughing.

One week later I was sitting on a bench by the front entrance to the school waiting for the Calabash bus. Maureen appeared, still wearing her cap. To my astonishment she knelt at my feet and looked at me fiercely. "Jenny, why you not come? Why you not come to my class?" She glared at me. "I love you, the children love you. Why you not come? You must come!"

I could not argue.

"I will come," I promised, and I did, taking with me a book of rhyme that I had bought for the class. I was sad when I returned to school in 2014 to find that Maureen was away on permanent sick leave. I never saw her again.

***

Nearly all the children in the school were affectionate and loving: many of the little ones liked to stroke the arms of volunteers. One day I visited the reception class and found all of the children singing. I listened, entranced, and then their teacher said, "You teach them an English song, Jenny."

I had always sung songs with my grandchildren and they had especially loved the ones with actions.

"In a cottage in a wood," I sang, miming the shape of a cottage and big trees in a wood. Fortunately, the teacher translated for me. I watched as 40 children repeated the whole song ending it, "Come little rabbit, come with me, / Happy we shall be". They all solemnly mimed cuddling their own little rabbit and yet again I had to blink back the tears.

***

So many memories come back to me as I write but one in particular stands out. March 6th 2013 was my grandson Mark's 18th birthday. I confessed to Zozo that I missed him and was feeling sad that I could not wish him a happy birthday.

"I have a phone card," I told Zozo, "but if I had rung from the hotel before school it would have been 5am in England." Not the time to ring a teenager!

"Jenny, you must speak to him," said Zozo. Without hesitation she selected 10 children. "Jenny will go with you to Zandi's office," she translated, then turned to me. "You can use your card to phone Mark from Zandi's office: she will not mind. Then the children will sing "Happy Birthday" to Mark. You must go now."

Zandi was the school secretary and in her office I dialled the lengthy list of numbers and waited for the recorded message. I could hardly believe it when eventually I heard the ringing tone. After what seemed ages, Mark answered.

"Hello", he said. He sounded very sleepy: of course it was still only 8am in the UK. Without any prompting the kids started to sing. When they finished I shouted, "Hello Mark! It's me, Jenny Gran! Happy birthday! I love you!"

One of the boys snatched the phone away from me.

"Mark… Happy birthday. I am a boy in South Africa, I love you too."

At that moment my two lives were united.

'because we are different'

Placement Outline: Jenny Baker
Isaac Booi: January 2014

Isaac Booi is delighted to have Jenny come and work at the school in the intermediate phase. Jenny will be working in Grade 4, 5 and 6 (ages 11,12, 13).

One of the great challenges in the education system is that children are required to learn in their second language (English), the higher up the grades they go, and they write their final exams in English.

As a result, the schools we work with value English teachers highly. It has been requested that Jenny work with the English teachers in these three Grades. There are two classes in each Grade. The teachers are being reshuffled a bit next year, so I cannot confirm exactly which teacher will be in which Grade..

It is requested that Jenny works in a team teaching approach, doing some observation and gives feedback, some model teaching, and some collaborative teaching.

All three these teachers have experience in working with volunteers, and are committed to supporting the volunteer, and using the time together to learn and share as much as possible.

Isaac Booi is sure that Jenny will be able to make a contribution to both the learners, and the teachers.

Jenny will work the closest with those teachers she worked with last year.

Everyone is excited to have Jenny Back.

CHAPTER TEN

TEACHING ALONE

When I arrived to volunteer again in 2014 I was anxious to see Zozo and Cynthia and rushed up the stairs to their classrooms. Zozo met me with a hug. "Oh Jenny, they said you were coming but I could not believe it." She took me over to her cupboard and opened it, smiling. "Look Jenny: I stayed after school to tidy it ready for your visit!" I laughed as I remembered opening the cupboard for the first time and the piles of books that had fallen out everywhere.

Next I went to Cynthia's classroom: she was not there but her class was.

"Where is Mrs Cadela?" I asked the children.

"She is not here, Mrs Jenny: she has gone on a course with some of the children. It is to train the leaders of the school; they will learn team-building."

In fact, Cynthia was away for my first four days. I took her lessons but there were no text or exercise books and no work was left so once again I had to resort to tales of "Becky and the Grandchildren". I learned that I could teach so much through stories about my little dog: she became the star of many lessons.

One day I went into school and there was no Cynthia and no Zozo either. Teaching Zozo's lessons was particularly hard that year, she had 4A, 4B and 4C. I helped her and found it was very confusing remembering what I had taught to which class. With both teachers away I had to decide what to do. I made my way to the Principal's office. He looked tired and despondent.

"Where is Zozo?" I asked. "Her classroom door is locked."

"I do not know, Jenny. I am sorry."

Together we walked to Zozo's room to find 40 children pushing and shoving in the corridor outside. Not only was the classroom locked but the key was missing.

"The caretaker has it," the Principal said – but no one could find the caretaker. I had often taught 40 kids on my own but even I could not contemplate teaching without a classroom. Eventually I was able to commandeer the "multipurpose room". Zozo had still not turned up so once again I found myself teaching alone.

Later I discovered that the caretaker had indeed had the key to Zozo's room but he had gone to the doctor and forgotten to tell the Principal. I also learnt that Zozo's little girl had been unwell and she too had forgotten to tell the Principal.

In 2014 I had to teach Cynthia's class on my own for the first four days. She had taken a group of children away on a leadership course. There was no work left for me. When she eventually returned I was happy to see her and I greeted her in our customary fashion.

"Good morning, Mrs Cynthia Cadela!"

"Good morning, Mrs Jenny Baker!" she replied, hugging me enthusiastically. "Since I last saw you, Jenny, I was chosen as a representative of netball and I have been to England! I saw the London Eye, the Tower, St Paul's Cathedral, Big Ben, the Houses of Parliament... I loved it all so much."

Despite my pleas to the teachers that they should tell me if they wanted me to teach alone they never did and often left the room without explanation. One day Zozo disappeared again, leaving me with one of the English students who had been teaching with us. I hastily looked through the textbooks and found a poem about a deserted beach. I read it twice out loud before telling the children to close their eyes tightly.

"Think about the rocks, the sea, the sand," I said. "Imagine being on your own on the beach."

After the lesson the children and the student left. The room was strangely silent and I sank exhaustedly onto a chair. It wobbled, one leg almost broken. Piles of tattered books, torn and musty, littered the shelves. The classroom walls were a dull khaki, reminiscent of the colour of soldiers' uniforms. I looked at the blackboard and shuddered, remembering my fingers scratching the surface as I tried to write with a minute piece of chalk.

I was tired, too tired to move. I wondered if I had achieved anything in the nine weeks I had then spent in the school. I was pleased with the five classrooms that had been painted by Boni and teams of children with the paint that we had bought, and also the huge, lidded dustbins we had given the school. These were tangible things… but I longed to leave something more lasting.

As I sat there thinking the door opened and a little girl entered. I remembered her from my Grade 4 lessons. I felt slightly guilty as I recollected her endless questions. I always had to bend down to listen to her tiny, bell-like voice. She came towards me, her eyes shining, and tugged at my sleeve. "Mrs Jenny, I want to write. Please may I write? I want to write a poem."

I did not hesitate.

"Of course you can write: come with me, we will find somewhere quiet."

It was impossible to find somewhere quiet in the school so I took her to the staffroom: I knew no one would mind. We sat down at a long table and I watched as she wrote. In a very short time she had finished and, without a word, passed her paper for me to read. I was amazed at the quality of her writing and so were the teachers who I showed it to. I still have her poem and feel it is very special. It was called 'I own the world'.

"You are a poet," I said to her. "Promise me that you will keep writing."

She nodded solemnly.

"What is your name?" I asked.

"My name is Hope," she replied. "My Mum says I can do anything if I want it enough."

I remembered then the poetry posters that I had brought with me from England, hoping that the school would use them. Quickly I got them from the cupboard.

"Please choose one, Hope," I said.

Slowly she read them all, finally picking out one by Sylvia Plath.

"You may have this," I said.

She was thrilled.

"My Mum will be so proud. Thank you, Mrs Jenny."

Hope, my little poetry girl

CHAPTER ELEVEN

THE BEST FRIENDS
READING AND WRITING CLUB

"Mrs Jenny, Mrs Jenny are we going to have our club?"

It was long break in 2015 and in front of me Hope was standing clutching her latest piece of writing. I took it with a smile, remembering the wonderful poem that she had written the previous year.

Together with three of Hope's classmates, I had formed a little club: "The Best Friends' Reading and Writing Club." Deliberately I had kept the numbers down: this would just be four friends, four nine year olds who loved reading and writing.

I had bought them a book by Michael Morpurgo and we had sat and read it outside in the lunch hour. I had many plans for our little club, the poetry and books we would explore, but they never materialised there were so many interruptions. At best we would meet for 20 minutes twice a week during long break. On the rare occasions when we did manage a meeting, I would be carried away by the children's enthusiasm. We would all be unconscious of time passing until one of them would suddenly say, "Mrs Jenny, the bell has gone, we must go to our classes."

In order to get to know the group better I had asked them at our first meeting to write something about themselves. Hope's account of her father's weekend visits had haunted me and looking into her large eyes I often wondered about her home life. Why was her father not at home? As she was in one of Cynthia's classes, I often got the chance to observe her. I was perturbed. In one lesson she was clearly not listening: eager hands shot up in response to Cynthia's questions but hers was never raised. She was in a world of her own, constantly tearing at her left hand with her fingernails. Eventually Cynthia got cross and drew attention to her, making her stand up. The questions and answers were in Xhosa but I could see that Hope was almost in tears. She sat down and after that began to raise her hand.

"Something is wrong with her," Cynthia whispered.

When the lesson finished I asked Hope to come with me. I didn't want to usurp Cynthia's authority so I said, "I was sad to see you behaving badly in Mrs Cadela's lesson. Is something wrong?"

"I miss my Dad," she said.

There was no time to ask more as the next class was due to begin but I remained concerned about her all day. She was usually so bright, imaginative and creative.

A few days later I was teaching with Cynthia and I saw someone hovering outside the door. Cynthia left the room briefly and then returned. "Hope's mother would like to talk with you, Jenny."

Together, Hope's mother and I went to the staffroom.

"I have come to thank you, Mrs Jenny, for what you have done for Hope. I know she is a bright girl; she loves the poem you gave her. It is on her wall. I am worried about her, I have three children and I am on my own."

The woman carried on talking, her eyes filling with tears as she told me her story. Hope's father had left, he was an alcoholic and working far away. Hope loved him; all her girls loved him. I bent forward so that I could hear her better, she was talking so quietly. "My eldest daughter was at university but she has left, I don't know where she is, I am frightened for her. I have no job; I have tried but I cannot get one. Can you help me, Mrs Jenny?"

I felt awful: this was not the first time I had been asked to assist someone in finding a job. I knew that it was beyond my power to help; I knew also that I must never offer help in the form of giving money. I muttered my apologies.

"Hope is a very special girl," I said at last. "Look after her."

We hugged and she went away. I returned to the classroom thinking about the huge problems faced by so many South Africans in the townships. There was so little I could do to help, and I thought often of my wish to give something tangible to the school. But although I did not know it then, I would eventually get my chance – and "my little poetry girl", Hope, would be there when I did.

Often I could not sleep at night, my mind was too full of the days' events. I would lie in my blue and white room at the Humewood, the sound of the waves crashing on the beach opposite. My thoughts would turn to the huge contrast between my life teaching in the south of England and my experiences in South Africa.

Although I had retired from teaching in 1999 I still remember the constant pressures of paperwork, targets and SATs. The staffroom in the large comprehensive school where I taught was always busy. Teachers rarely had time to sit and chat. In contrast at Isaac Booi as I have mentioned before no-one rushed to their lessons when the bell went and all meetings seemed to be held during lesson time, leaving classes of children unattended. There was no money for supply teachers.

The Best Friends Reading and Writing Club

I own the world
My story.

I own the world
But the trees talk to me and say
"You don't own the world"

I don't care like it or not I own the
world. The wind talks to me and
says
"don't lie to your self you ain't
gonna own the world"

"I don't understand" I said to myself
The rock shows up and say
"You will understand one day"

I went home, I lay on my bed
And started to think
I went to the sea and I said
"I understand now"
The rock said
"I knew you would understand"

Written by: Lithemba Makosi

Hope

CHAPTER TWELVE

A VISIT TO THE TOWNSHIP

I asked Cynthia and Zozo if it would be possible to visit the homes of some of my pupils. They readily agreed.

"You must take presents when you visit," Cynthia said.

"Like what?" I asked.

"Rice, sugar, tea, coffee: the parents will be grateful for anything," she answered.

I remember that morning so well. Of course I had travelled through townships every day on my way to school but actually visiting peoples' homes was very different. I was struck by the extremes of poverty: the houses made from wood, cardboard and corrugated iron yet I could also see TV aerials everywhere. We were in the heart of the township; on the outskirts new brick Mandela houses were being built but I was told that people were loath to move to better housing as they were so used to the close communal life of the inner township.

Cynthia led me to the first house where a large boy from her class greeted me. He looked immensely proud as he introduced me to his father; his mother, I learned, had died. A very old lady lay on a couch, clearly unwell. Cynthia turned to the father speaking powerfully and with much emotion. "I have chosen your son's home for Jenny to visit," she said. "Before he came to our school he was a bad boy. He was expelled from his first school."

I looked at the boy: there were tears in his eyes and his face was contorted.

"Your son was in a lot of trouble," Cynthia continued, still speaking to his father. "But since he has been at Isaac Booi School he has tried hard and he has improved. This is why I have chosen him. Now he must continue to do well."

The boy looked sheepish but he nodded and said, "Yes, Mrs Cadela: I will try hard. Thank you, Mrs Jenny, for coming to my home."

I blinked away the tears as I gave my gifts to his frail grandmother. Cynthia looked on, smiling. "She really does care about the kids in her class," I thought to myself. I had had my doubts when I first arrived at Isaac Booi: Cynthia had seemed very strict, constantly shouting orders at the children. Later I learned that she was a single mother, trying her best to bring up her two boys on her own, and when I met them they were polite, charming and very gentle and kind to their three-year-old cousin who lived with them.

Just inside the township

A warm welcome

A girl greeted us at the next home we visited. She seemed young to me and yet she was single-handedly caring for eight children, only three of whom were hers. She showed us into the house, part of it converted into a makeshift chapel. Musical instruments lay around and two toddlers sat banging drums. There was a small cooker and a table. The walls were brick: far better than many of the township homes. I felt so humbled by the welcome we received. I admired those hardworking women and reflected that it could have been me but for an accident of birth.

After our visit we emerged into the sunshine and walked past Ahtana's Tavern. Four men were lounging around. I got the impression that women did the majority of the work. Everywhere we went we encountered small businesses run by women; I was told that there was one hairdresser for every four women. We went inside one of their shops and the owner greeted us warmly. She was an extremely large glamorous lady; she wore a white dress held up by skimpy straps. There were funeral parlours one every street but we did not visit any of them. Finally, we passed a shebeen and I remembered evenings spent with the other volunteers, drinking beer and eating simple food whilst an African band played and sang. The band was obviously for the benefit of tourists, but many locals also went. I had read that in the past shebeens were operated illegally by women in a revival of the African tradition that assigned the role of brewing alcohol to women. During the Apartheid era shebeens were crucial meeting places for activists. Today shebeens are legal and an integral part of township culture.

Local entrepeneur

A little further on some more women stood under the shade of a tree selling clothes that were piled on the ground. The countless shops and stalls testified to the entrepreneurial spirit of the people.

CHAPTER THIRTEEN

THE 'LIBRARY'

The library at Isaac Booi was a large metal storage container, brightly painted on the outside by previous volunteer students. It looked very inviting but I never saw it open. After three weeks in the school I finally asked if I could see inside it. Eventually a key was found. I walked in to discover scores of white plastic boxes, neatly stored and labelled by age and subject. It was hot, stiflingly hot! I opened some of the boxes and the illusion of order was dispelled: the contents were jumbled. Some boxes labelled as being for 12-14 year olds contained hardback picture books. Sorting the library would be a huge task, I thought to myself. Maybe someday future volunteers would do it.

"Why don't the children use all these lovely books?" I asked Cynthia later. I felt sad that the boxes were untouched and the books seemed never to have been read.

"It is because of CAPS, Jenny. We are always so busy, there is not time to use the books. The children have to do all their reading from the CAPS textbook."

CAPS, I discovered, was a national curriculum assessment policy for Grades R-12. It was incredibly complicated. The teachers were bound by law to follow what had to be taught on a term-to-term basis. I felt sympathetic: having been a teacher myself I remembered getting my pupils ready for SATS and the pressure that had imposed.

However, the thought of those books lying unused stayed with me even when I returned to England. I vowed that when I went back to Isaac Booi on my third visit I would try and do something about them. One of the classrooms in the school was known as the multipurpose room and I would often look around it, visualising a beautiful library. Unlike the rest of the school it was light and airy, its furniture unbroken, its windows intact. Some loving care had gone into this area and there were bright pictures on the walls, a legacy (I suspected) left by previous volunteers. I knew that my dream of creating a library in the school was naïve: I had books, but no room and no librarian. Also, resources didn't always seem to be valued. I had only once been inside the school's stockroom and what I had seen had saddened, shocked and angered me: piles of books littered the floor, so much so there was hardly room to walk.

On the way home that day I questioned Paul about this.

"You see, Jenny, these people have had nothing for so long it is natural that they are loath to throw anything away. The Principal must give permission before anything is disposed of."

This would explain all the broken furniture that, although clearly useless, was retained, cluttering the school, much of it laying on the flat roofs.

But despite the difficulties, the idea of a library would not go away. Those little "bees" in my head just kept buzzing. I decide to suggest to Cynthia that we sort and clean the books and then distribute them to classes around the school, but she clearly thought that was not a good idea.

"Jenny, there is nowhere to store the books in the classrooms, there are no cupboards to lock them in. They would get stolen."

Secretly I almost wished that they would get stolen: at least then they would be used. "We would love to have a library," Cynthia said at last. "But where could we put it?"

Over the weekend I could not get Cynthia's question out of my mind. I went back to school on Monday determined to find a solution to the problem. When I ran into Mike the caretaker he looked tired and rather anxious - I hated bothering him but I needed his help. I knew that he was just a volunteering as a caretaker and that he did not get paid. He was the father of one of the pupils, "my son is a great rugby player" he had told me proudly.

"Mike, please may I have a look in one of the storerooms?" I asked him.

He produced an enormous bunch of keys, fumbling with them as he searched for the right one. It took ages but finally the door opened... and what I saw made me gasp. For a moment I was speechless. I was prepared for chaos but this was beyond anything I could possibly have imagined. The room was packed from floor to ceiling with computers, keyboards, monitors, the floor littered with broken objects. I felt sure that there must be at least 50 of everything, plus huge tables, lawn mowers and paint.

"Nothing works," said Mike, shaking his head sadly.

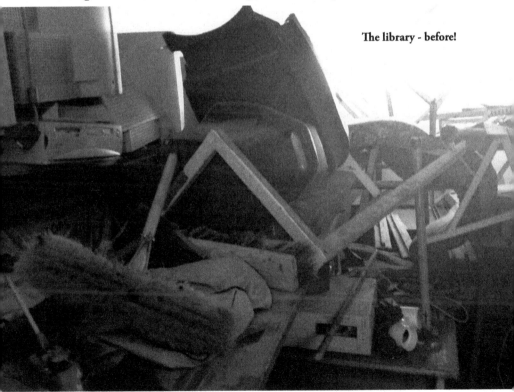

The library - before!

Suddenly I knew that this room was the answer to the question that had been haunting me. This would be the library. There was a large window at the end of the room and it was cool and secure.

I hardly slept at all that night. How would I clear the room? Who would clean the books? Most importantly, who would be the librarian? Next morning, I saw Cynthia.

"Good morning, Mrs Cynthia Cadela."

"Good morning, Mrs Jenny Baker."

We laughed and hugged.

"Cynthia, I must talk to you, it is urgent."

We sat on the stone seat under the huge willow tree and I told her about my plan. She agreed immediately.

"Yes Jenny, we must do it."

***

The next morning the Calabash bus was full: 11 students from Sheffield Hallam University in England had arrived. I sat next to one of them, Sarah, and learned that she and three of her friends were going to be volunteering at Isaac Booi. I told her about my plans for the library.

"We'll help," she assured me.

Soon we were all talking, the students' enthusiasm matching my own as ideas tumbled back and forth. Once at the school I showed them the storeroom: they were shocked but undaunted.

"We'll paint a huge sun on the end wall: it will be the first thing the children see when they come into the room," said Sarah.

Together we went to the Principal's office and told him about our plans. He readily gave his assent and smiled when we asked if we could use his computer: we needed to look online and find a firm who would clear the room. We quickly found that the Principal's computer was not working. "I always have problems with it," he said. I felt so sorry for him.

Students from Sheffield Hallam University lend a hand

Returning to Zandi the secretary's office, we resorted to South Africa's equivalent of the Yellow Pages. After several phone calls I finally found someone willing to do the work. He promised that he would not charge us but he would not give us anything for the contents either. I had hoped to get something for the scrap metal but it proved impossible and it was imperative that we clear the room quickly. I felt nervous as I agreed: I did not even know the guy.

That evening I was invited for a meal at the home of a Rotarian I had met the previous year. Over supper I told her about my plans and the telephone conversation.

"Jenny, my friend's husband runs a clearing service," she said. "I will call him."

She did so immediately and passed the phone to me. I heard laughter.

"You spoke to me this morning!" the voice at the other end exclaimed. "I have your email; I will definitely do the job but I cannot come until next week. I will be with you on Wednesday."

I had no alternative so I agreed, but I was worried. Friday was to be my last day at the school meaning I had just five days to make a library! I was reminded of "Challenge Anneka", a TV programme from the late 80s in which Anneka Rice was given a challenge and had just three days to complete it. This was certainly "Challenge Jenny!" At the age of 78 I felt that I really should be at home knitting rather than trying to accomplish a seemingly impossible task in a South African township. However, I don't like knitting and I was determined that I would make a library for the children whatever the odds.

I had several great assets. One was Cynthia, my friend and team teacher: she was a feisty, determined lady and shared my vision.

"You should just see Cynthia on the netball court!" Paul had laughingly told me.

Another special lady, Miss January, was also enthusiastic. I had known and respected her since my first visit in 2013 but I didn't actually teach with her until 2015. We had gone on to develop a natural rapport and I enjoyed sharing her lessons. The children obviously loved her, especially those in the choir that she skilfully conducted (she herself was a wonderful singer). I had no hesitation in telling her about my plans for the library and she immediately gave her support.

My third asset was the students from Sheffield Hallam University. Realistically I knew that the library could not possibly be finished before I had to leave and I was thankful that I could hand the project over to young people as enthusiastic as myself.

As I walked around the school I often met parents who offered me wide smiles and friendly greetings. My contributions to the parents' meetings had obviously been appreciated but I was unsure about how much support I would get with the library project. I estimated that there were hundreds of books in the container. They would all need cleaning, having accumulated the dust of many years.

I confessed my fears to Cynthia. "The books all need clearing and sorting, there are hundreds of them, how can we manage?"

"Do not worry, Jenny: the mamas will come, they will do it."

I was incredulous.

"Are you sure, Cynthia? Won't they want money?"

"I am sure, Jenny. I will tell them to do it for the love of their children, not for money."

Still I was doubtful, but on the Monday morning of my final week, there they were: 16 mothers waiting for me outside the door of the staffroom. We went inside and sat around in a circle: an old lady from England and mothers and grandmothers from the township. I reflected that we were not so very different in that moment.

"This is our challenge," I told them. The reality of the task sank in as I explained that every book would have to be cleaned. "Come with me to the container please," I said.

They were strong women and very quickly carried dozens of plastic boxes filled with books to the staffroom. I rushed to get the brightly coloured buckets that I had bought previously. The school had no dusters or cleaning cloths but the receptionist at Humewood Hotel had given me a large, old towel that I cut into pieces and soon the mamas were busy cleaning the books.

Every available surface was covered. I was concerned that the staff would be cross but no one seemed to mind. With so much going on I was worried that I was missing lessons and once again I confided in Cynthia.

"Jenny, you must do the library, it is important. Do not worry."

All my problems seemed small compared with one huge question: who would run the library? I was cross with myself: I had been so involved with the practical problems that I had neglected this one vital point. What use was a room full of books if there was no one to take charge?

Yet again I sought out Cynthia.

"Who can we get to run the library?" I asked her. She thought for a moment.

"Ask Thembisa."

"Thembisa? You mean Thembisa who is volunteering in the office?"

"Yes, you must ask Thembisa."

I was amazed. Why had I not thought of Thembisa? We had met in 2014 and I had been immediately impressed. She had come into the staffroom whilst I was sitting marking, a slim and beautiful woman with a serious look on her face. I learned that she was about to start work as a social worker for two schools - no wonder she looked serious.

In 2015 I was surprised to see her working on the computer in the secretary's office. "I lost my job, Jenny, there was no money. So here I am volunteering, helping Zandi with secretarial work."

I found Thembisa in the office and her face lit up when she saw me.

"Thembisa, you know we are making a library for the children?"

She nodded.

"We cannot run a library without a librarian, please can you help?"

There was moment's pause. I was frightened: without a librarian all my plans would be pointless. My heart was racing…but the pause was only momentary.

"Yes Jenny, I will do it! But I don't know how to run a library. Please, will you help me?"

I flung my arms around her and we hugged.

"Oh Thembisa, thank you! We will make it the best school library in the Eastern Cape! I will make sure that you have some training."

Paul had told me previously that there was a librarian in one of his other schools who would be willing to help.

Back in the staffroom the mothers were still cleaning. One was obviously the leader and strangely her name was also Thembisa. I had seen her around the school and watched her now as she cleaned: she was thorough and determined.

"Thembisa," I said, "thank you for all you are doing. We are going to need a very special person to clean the library when it opens - will you do it?"

She smiled broadly. "Yes," she replied.

I was so relieved: in one day I had found the two most important people.

CHAPTER FOURTEEN

FROM DREAM TO REALITY

My days in South Africa started very early: I was usually up at 5am and liked to walk on the beach before breakfast at 6.30. It gave me time to think about the day ahead. As I walked on the second day of the library project, I planned, the mamas would continue cleaning the books and the students could start classifying them. I knew that there would be many books too old and damaged for the new library so I planned to give them to the parent helpers.

When I arrived at school I met Cynthia in the staffroom. We talked over our plans for the following day.

"As soon as the room has been cleared, the mamas will clean the room and then they will start painting," Cynthia said calmly. "The library will be finished before you leave."

Impossible, I thought, looking at the mamas and the huge piles of books.

At 9.30am Zandi, the secretary, came into the staffroom. "Jenny, you are wanted on the phone," she announced.

My heart sank: it could only be the man who was coming to clear the room. Was he ringing to cancel? I picked up the phone.

"Hello Jenny. I have a gap in my schedule. I can come to the school now instead of tomorrow. I have a 20-minute slot. I will be with you in 30 minutes: please make sure the room is cleared and that everything is outside ready for me."

I was terrified, I felt completely helpless. How could we possibly empty the room in 30 minutes? It was impossible! I wanted to run away! I felt sick!

Ludwe, the fourth member of my teaching team, was in the office and must have seen the look of alarm on my face.

"Leave it with me, Jenny," he said coolly. "You know I will not let you down."

I knew Ludwe well and he had often come to my rescue. Now I watched amazed as he organised scores of boys outside the crowded storeroom. Soon they had formed a human chain to pass the junk out, many of them singing and dancing as they balanced computers precariously on their heads. On and on they went, walking past me as I watched helpless and terrified: there were no health and safety rules in South African township schools and I feared there would be an accident. Many of the boys seemed far too small to be carrying so much weight.

"Oh, what have we done?" I said to Cynthia, who had joined me to watch.

"Don't worry Jenny, it will be okay."

When the removal man arrived I hardly dared look: his trailer seemed too small for such a huge load. But in half an hour the task was finished.

With Cynthia I returned to the room. It was still half full yet some boys were already cleaning. I knew that endless forms should be filled in before anything was thrown away but I was in too deep, I could not go back. The boys worked on and on. The corridor was lined with junk but by 12.30pm the "library" was at last clear. Cynthia and I collapsed laughing, hugging each other as we looked at the empty space.

"We are miracle women!" she said.

"Yes, we are miracle women," I agreed.

Miracle woman!

I looked at the empty shelves, imagining them lined with books. As I stood there, four of the mothers entered, buckets in hand, and immediately started scrubbing. I clearly wasn't needed. I returned to the staffroom exhausted and sat down.

When I opened my eyes it was to find Hope standing before me.

"Mrs Jenny, it is time for our club!"

I sighed.

"I'm afraid we cannot have the club today: Mrs Jenny is so busy with the new library. But you can come and help me."

She agreed happily and we began to sort the piles of books, but not before we had our photos taken together. There was something very apt about my "little poetry girl" being there at that moment on that incredible day and I thought about how the library might inspire Hope long after I had left Isaac Booi.

It was now early afternoon and time to begin the decorating. Three mamas and a grandmother were waiting to start and I was thankful that I had brought paint the previous day. But then disaster struck.

"Where is the sandpaper?" one of them asked.

I felt very embarrassed: with so much to do I had forgotten it.

"It does not matter, we can manage without it," one of the mamas said.

But the oldest lady contradicted her firmly. "No the job must be done properly, we need sandpaper."

When I returned half an hour later it was to find the grandmother standing on a ladder, a piece of sandpaper in her hand. She beamed at me as she rubbed down the walls. How they managed to find that sandpaper I do not know....

I wanted to stay after school and carry on with decorating but the Principal would not allow it. "No, Jenny I cannot let you do it. A teacher in another area was murdered in her classroom after the school closed. It is too dangerous."

However, the next morning I arrived at the school only to find that the first coat of paint had already been completed: Thembisa and her friend had evidently stayed late. Had they managed to get permission from the Principal, I wondered? I was very touched but I had no time to thank them: I had to find the students and return to the minibus. We were going shopping for the library.

It was an exciting morning. The students bought green, woven rugs and I got dried flowers and brightly patterned cushions. By the time we returned to school the second coat of paint was completed. I was thrilled, and happy to leave the finishing touches to the students who had such wonderful plans for it.

After school I went to the photographers at the Pick and Pay shopping centre and collected the thank you cards I had ordered for the mamas. I made sure to sign every one of them.

Assembly on my last morning was an emotional one. The Principal asked me to speak but before I could do so all the kids started shouting: "Viva Jenny! Viva the library!"

The noise intensified, the phrases repeated over and over. The teachers were clapping wildly.

"Viva the students! Viva the library!" cried the kids.

The chorus went on and on, louder and louder, until finally the Principal stepped forward and held up his hand for quiet. He dismissed the children and I walked back to the staffroom. Outside the mamas were waiting. I gave each one of them a card and thanked them sincerely. Two of them grumbled: they wanted money.

"I told you that you must do this because you love your children, it is not for money," Cynthia told them, clearly cross.

Nevertheless, they were happy to stand in a line and have their photograph taken.

That day there were more and more photographs, as well as countless hugs and handshakes. I gave Thembisa a beautiful pot and Mike a bottle of whiskey.

For the rest of the morning I showed small groups of children around the room that was to become their library. Their eyes widened in amazement when they saw the brightly painted blue walls and the books on the shelves. Finally, I stood their alone, imagining the sun that the students planned to paint: already they had started working on the blue sky. My job was finished. I took one last look round, imagining it complete with books, pictures, cushions and rugs. I wished that I could be at the official opening. Sighing, I left and locked the door.

***

The library - After!

Two weeks later my friend and fellow volunteer Susan sent me pictures of the official opening of the library. I was thrilled. It looked as wonderful as I had imagined.

The first one showed Cynthia cutting a ribbon strung across the door. There were balloons everywhere. Other pictures showed the mural that the students had painted; it completely covered the wall under the window and showed the sun shining invitingly. The students had done a wonderful job. The room looked friendly and inviting and even better than I possibly could have imagined.

In an email to me Cynthia later wrote "so we are all continuing with the library that is there for life. That's a promise that I personally give to you and I will keep."

Finished at last!

• CHAPTER FIFTEEN •

THE ACCIDENT

It happened one afternoon in February 2014 as I was walking along the pavement outside the Pick and Pay shopping centre. With no warning I found myself on the ground, the pain in my wrist agonising. I lay there stunned. Had I tripped? A car drew up and a young man who later told me he was a student got out. "Are you okay?" he asked, peering down at me.

"No, I'm not," I murmured. "I think I have broken my wrist."

Somehow he managed to get me up.

"Where are you staying?" he asked. "I don't think you've done any real harm."

But I knew he was wrong. The pain was intensifying.

He drove me back to the hotel where everyone gathered round and decided that I must be taken to the hospital. My friend and fellow volunteer Liz was very concerned. "I'll come with you, Jenny," she said.

My memories of that first hospital visit are very blurred. I was seen quickly and a young doctor gave me an injection. "I think you've broken it," he said, a diagnosis which an x-ray confirmed. Finally, a consultant came in. "I will operate tomorrow," he said. "You can go back to your hotel and return to the hospital at 6am. Do not eat anything after 9 o'clock tonight."

After a restless night I went back to the hospital accompanied by Christine, another volunteer. I was glad to have company. We waited and waited and waited. The hours passed. Finally, I persuaded Christine to go. Just as well: it was not until 2pm that I was given an anaesthetic.

I woke up feeling very sick. My arm was attached to a drip and I was immobile. I shouted for help but no one came for what seemed like an eternity. Eventually a nurse came and begrudgingly cleaned me up. She looked very fierce and I thought how the ward was a sharp contrast to the warmth and the friendliness I had experienced in the school.

There were more problems when an orderly brought a tray with food on it. I was lying flat on my back so she balanced it precariously on my stomach. I was totally helpless: I certainly could not sit up to eat. Eventually someone took the tray away and I fell asleep. When I woke, it was to see four black faces looking at me.

"We are your family in South Africa, Jenny, we have come to see you."

It was Cynthia with three teachers from the school. I was touched that they had driven from the township.

I dozed off and on through the night. No nurses came near me until 6 o'clock the next morning when one helped me to the bathroom and washed me. At 11am I was told I could go home. Feeling very hungry and rather faint - somehow I had missed breakfast - a nurse helped me to dress and I made my way down the corridor. In the reception there was a small café where I bought a biscuit and ate it quickly. A receptionist then called me over and asked me for my name.

"You pay," she said sternly, thrusting a bill into my hand. "You pay."

That phrase came up continually in the week that followed. I had to pay for blood tests, x-rays, nursing, consultants and so on and so on. It amounted to thousands of rands, but (fortunately) only just over £200.

Finally, my taxi came and I was very relieved to be back at the Humewood. I slipped thankfully into bed and slept. That evening Christine and Liz cut up my food and the next day they walked with me along the promenade. I managed amazingly well with my right wrist out of action and was back at the school the following day. Jackie, the receptionist at the Humewood, put my earrings in for me every day. "Reporting for earring duty," she would say when I walked into reception each morning. It was characteristic of her; she spent hours helping me with my insurance claim and was unfailingly kind throughout my stay at the hotel.

My biggest worry as I had lain in the hospital bed was how I would put my bra on. This I solved by first fastening it and then pulling it up over my bum! Another worry was that I would be unable to drive if I returned to England when I had planned, so I decided to stay in South Africa for an extra week – first making the staff promise that there would not be another leaving ceremony.

Still the bills kept coming. Paul took me in his car to the hospital to pay the final one. On the way he told me about his neighbour, a man who ran a small business that had got into difficulties. Money was tight and the man had to stop paying health insurance. In the months that followed his daughter became seriously ill and was taken into hospital. Her life was saved but Paul's neighbour had to sell his house in order to pay the bills. Sitting in that car I felt so thankful for our National Health Service.

• CHAPTER SIXTEEN •

PEOPLE AND PLACES

Port Elizabeth has a long promenade and I spent many happy hours walking and marvelling at the blue sea in the January sun. At weekends families congregated on the beach. Usually black and white groups were separated, but often I would see boys of every colour playing football together. Kite surfing was another popular pastime and on one occasion I remember looking on amazed as a man flew past me. His dog ran back and forth as the kite travelled at tremendous speed. I began to grow anxious, fearing that the dog would die from exhaustion, but it looked deliriously happy.

The walkway was long and it got less crowded as I neared the university. I was always wary of walking alone. Often I would travel back on the taxi-buses that ran between Port Elizabeth and the university all day long. There was no timetable but I could always hear one coming. A boy would stand on the dashboard shouting furiously for passengers until it was full. There seemed to be no limit to the number of people a taxi would carry and they were renowned for being dangerous although I never saw any accidents. (I think the long distance ones were riskier.) I was usually the only white passenger and for eight rands could travel anywhere in Port Elizabeth. I always loved these journeys with African music blaring out. The drivers were friendly and they always stopped right outside the Humewood for me.

The Sunday market was the highlight of the week. There were countless stalls selling beautifully carved animals; some of them were huge, many were carved from stone. The stallholders who made them came from Zimbabwe and I got to know them well. Some of them were also there during the week and they would often be setting up their stalls as I returned from my morning walk on the beach. They would shout after me, "Good morning Jenny Gran, come and buy from me!" I did, and my three beautiful carved elephants remind me daily of Port Elizabeth.

Opposite our hotel was the huge swimming pool that I had visited on my first day. Beside it there was a cocktail bar, very ornate with plush armchairs and shining tables. A long balcony overlooked the pool and we volunteers would often sit there sipping our drinks. The pool always looked so inviting and I enjoyed lying on the white plastic sofas at its edge after a day's teaching. It was so very different from the township. As Paul had said when we first arrived, "Your visit will be a tale of two cities."

He was so right.

EDWARD

I met Edward in 2014: he had a hairdresser's shop in a very fashionable tourist mall and I often saw him standing outside, a small, rotund balding man touting for business. One day, feeling rather scared, I asked him if he could cut my hair.

"Yees, yees my darling," he responded enthusiastically. "Yees, yees, I cut your hair, you come in!"

Within seconds I was sitting at a mirror and Edward, having washed my hair, was cutting enthusiastically, turning my head this way and that singing and talking as he worked.

"I don't want it too short," I cautioned. Edward ignored me, his scissors moving swiftly and deftly. Then he started to dance as he worked. He clearly knew what he was doing. Finally, he ran his fingers through my hair, drying it in minutes.

"It is finished, my darling," he cried. "You look beautiful!"

I could not agree that I looked beautiful but I was amazed: he had managed to tame my unruly hair and without any instruction from me had styled it just as I wanted.

The next day I returned to his shop and Edward coloured my hair perfectly. So much so that Christine immediately went off to book an appointment for herself.

One of the first things I did when I arrived on my next trip was to look for Edward. My hair badly needed cutting after two weeks backpacking. I was devastated when I reached his shop only to find it closed. I asked many people but no one knew where he was. Finally, I went to the Pick and Pay centre.

"Do you know a good hairdresser?" I asked my friend in the photography shop.

"Yes, there is one upstairs on the second floor," she replied.

I went up and to my surprise there was Edward standing outside the door.

"Hello my darling," he said, "you are back! I will cut your hair!"

Edward's new shop was full of people all talking animatedly about politics. Again he danced and sang as he worked and his new assistant clapped enthusiastically when he had finished.

"You look beautiful, my darling," he said.

MARCELLE

I met Marcelle on my third visit to Port Elizabeth.

Jane, one of my fellow volunteers on that trip, was a scientist and when we first arrived she was planning some science experiments for her classes. One evening at dinner she told us about her trip to the pharmacy in the mall. "I bought so many strange things," she said, "the pharmacist was staring at me in amazement. 'What on earth are you getting all this for?' she asked. I told her that I was volunteering in a township school."

It turned out that the pharmacist, Marcelle a white South African lady, was also a volunteer.

"She adopted a school 13 years ago and she seems to be an amazing woman. You must meet her, Jenny," Jane urged.

The next time I went to Pick and Pay I asked for Marcelle. She appeared from the back of the counter and when I explained who I was she hugged me enthusiastically. She was middle-aged and very attractive; her hair was thick and wavy and her eyes sparkled as she talked non-stop, telling me about "her" school.

"Thirteen years ago," she said, "I had a customer with diabetes. He had to visit often for his prescriptions. He was a black man and he said his wife was the headmistress of a township school. He invited me to visit and I went the following week. What I saw that day changed my life. I adopted that school."

"Look at this," she said getting some large sheets of paper out of her bag. "This afternoon I will go to the school. This is a list of what must be done!"

I read Marcelle's list, marvelling. It was headed "Things to remember today" and began:

1. Tidy and clean the Principal's desk.

2. Pick up all litter from the playground.

3. Check and count all the pencils.

On and on it went.

"The teachers are my friends," Marcelle told me. "Jenny, please come and visit my school."

I promised that I would try.

Sometimes life is stranger than fiction. When I returned to Isaac Booi in 2015 I had looked forward to meeting Boni, the chairman of the governors, again. However, in the first few days I did not see her at all.

"Where is Boni?" I asked the school secretary. She did not answer my question directly but promised to telephone Boni and tell her that I had arrived. The next day Boni was waiting for me in the staffroom and we hugged. She looked rather solemn. We sat down and she began to talk: "Jenny, I will be chair of the governors for just three more weeks. My children are now at a smaller school and it is wonderful. A white lady has been helping the school for 13 years: it is amazing what she has done. You must come and visit."

I discovered that Boni's children had in fact transferred to Marcelle's school. Of course I had to visit. On the day I was accompanied by my fellow volunteers and some English students who were training to be teachers. We were welcomed by the principle and Boni; Marcelle was at work. The school was hugely impressive, clean and tidy, with not a speck of litter anywhere. Everywhere I saw evidence of Marcelle's enthusiasm: new tables and chairs, a well-stocked library etc., etc.

Now, in 2017, I am still emailing Marcelle and learning more about her work. She was and is hugely energetic, constantly using her charm to persuade owners of factories and large firms to support her work. A team of ladies knit dolls and on one occasion she brought flip-flops for every child in the school and distributed prom dresses to the older girls. In 2016 she was short listed for Port Elizabeth's woman of the year award. She has lost none of her enthusiasm over the years and I have gained a friend.

LIZ

I met Liz on my second visit to South Africa, she was slim and wiry with a determined look in her eyes. I learned that she was to be volunteering at the Emmanuel Care Advice Centre. By the end of our first conversation I knew that she was a kindred spirit and we still remain friends.

I have great respect for Liz, she quickly took Emmanuel to her heart and has returned to Port Elizabeth on three occasions. We met again in 2015 when she spent half her time staying at the Humewood and the other half living with Mama Arche in the Township. Mama Arche was one of the volunteer caregivers at Emmanuel, her husband, a pastor, had been tragically murdered some years previously.

The care centre is an amazing place; it was started in 2004 by a very committed social worker with the help of several black volunteer caregivers from the community. Its aim was to visit Township homes and offer support links between the community and available services. A crèche was set up to help look after forty-eight orphans and vulnerable children. I'm not sure when or how Calabash got involved, but I do know that Liz was the perfect volunteer for Emmanuel with her background in youth and community work, plus environmental and grass-roots projects. Initially the care centre was funded by stipends from the government, but these stopped and it is now totally dependent on donations. Liz was in Port Elizabeth for the first three months of 2017 renting a flat and a car and driving between the city and Emmanuel "the women care-givers have become my family". She told me "they are incredible, their perseverance and dedication while trying to feed themselves is remarkable." Emmanuel has its own Facebook page and Liz is now the international secretary. I feel privileged to have volunteered with her.

PEOPLE AND PLACES:
AN ETHICAL VOLUNTEERING FIRM

Many people have asked me if I would like to volunteer again and the answer must be 'yes', although age and time are against me. I would encourage anyone reading this book to volunteer. I recommend 'People and Places,' the firm is based at Faversham in Kent and one the award for responsible tourism campaigning at the World Tourism Awards in 2013. It works with partner organisations in developing countries. Formed in 2005 their first volunteer went out to South Africa in 2006 working with the Calabash Trust. All company profit is covenanted by charitable purposes through Travel Pledge and they aim to enable volunteers and local communities to gain mutual benefits through sharing skills.

THE CALABASH BUS

The Calabash bus picked us up at 7am every morning. We volunteers would clamber on armed with marking, visual aids and packed lunches. Often the journeys were long, people had to be collected from many schools. At the end of the day we would wearily climb back onto the bus sometimes too tired to talk. The drivers were always punctual, courteous and full of fun. They played a big part in our volunteering experience, telling us about their lives in the townships. They became our friends. We talked about our days. I often wondered what they thought of us.

I particularly enjoyed sitting next to Nelson when he was driving. He regularly took tourists into the Township. He was passionate about Fairtrade Tourism & the work of the Calabash Trust. We had long discussions about the political situation in South Africa. I was aware of his close friendship with Paul. One day he told me about their first meeting at a youth gathering. It was 1989 and the country was still under Apartheid so a social gathering including coloureds, whites and blacks was very unusual.

"It was when our friendship started," Nelson told me, " I was very impressed with the way Paul was broad minded about the situation in South Africa. He was completely against racism. I lost contact with him when he left PE to go to university in Cape Town. When he returned to Port Elizabeth I did not know he was back but I read about him in our daily newspaper The Herald. The article was about how he and his wife Thandi had started Calabash Tours. I decided to visit him and that was when he asked me to work for him. I joined Calabash a year later."

Apartheid did not condone friendships between black and white. He was born and bred in the township and is passionate about Fairtrade tourism. He takes tourists into the township and shares with them his knowledge of history and politics; I learned so much from him in our conversations as we journeyed to and from the school.

CHAPTER SEVENTEEN

WANDERLUST

Ever since I was a small girl I have suffered from wanderlust. At eight years old I often caught the 227 bus from Bickley in Kent to Chislehurst. There I wandered over the common and through the woods with my friend, Barbara. Like me, she was an only child and the Kent countryside offered freedom from the roads of semi-detached houses where we both lived. As we got older we explored further, catching the train to Shoreham and SevenOaks. In that bygone age children were allowed to have adventures.

When I was planning to visit South Africa it was therefore natural that my thoughts turned to what I wanted to do after I had finished volunteering. I asked the advice of a Saga rep.

"How about a safari?" she suggested, and recommended Shiduli on the Karongwe Game Reserve.

I took her advice. After my four weeks teaching I left the Humewood Hotel in Port Elizabeth at 5am, touched that Irene and Andrew had got up to wave me off. Stepping off the tiny plane some time later at Hoedspruit Airport, I was amazed and charmed by the small landing strip: it was more like a miniature theme park than an airport. Landscaped gardens with pools, streams and gravel made a perfect backdrop for beautifully crafted statues of animals. There was a single check-in desk and no conveyor belt for our luggage: we just picked it up. A man was holding up a board with my name on it. "I am here to take you to Shiduli," he said, beaming.

We travelled through wild countryside with the Drakensburg Mountains in the distance. Arriving at the lodge I was met by Sam, my guide. He was reassuringly large, dressed in immaculate shorts, shirt and a bush hat.

"Come, Jenny: I will show you to your bungalow."

We walked through the grounds, past a swimming pool with a fountain, blue loungers and an inviting bar. It was blissfully quiet. After passing rows of neatly thatched cottages we reached a bungalow standing on its own. Sam produced a large key and opened the door. I stood amazed.

"This is the honeymoon suite," he said, smiling, "I hope you will be comfortable here."

I looked at the huge bed, wide enough for four people. It had an ornately carved headboard, four posts and draperies in white muslin. The sheets and pillows were in virginal white; the lighting was muted. Tiny flowers shaped like a heart spelled out "WELCOME" on the coverlet. I felt excited yet sad and a little uncomfortable. The luxury contrasted hugely with the township and I also missed Bob, my husband. The lounge with its two chairs and the bathroom with its double sink accentuated my loneliness.

Venturing outside, I found a second shower and a whirlpool! It was hot and I was tired after my journey so I quickly changed into a swimming costume and minutes later was dipping my feet in the pool. I relaxed thinking of the wildlife that I would soon be seeing. I closed my eyes, revelling in the peace. Suddenly I heard screams and a huge baboon swung from a tree in front of me, closely followed by others barking and grunting. They leapt from branch to branch and surrounded me. I was terrified! Luckily only my feet and legs were in the pool. I scrambled out and fled to the lodge, slamming the door behind me, my heart thudding. How I missed Bob.

Sadly, I never ventured into the pool again, nor did I see the baboons. That evening I made my way up to the dining room where a large party of Saga guests were sitting. A lone table had been laid in the middle of the room with a single napkin and cutlery for one. The waiter indicated that I should sit there. I remained there for a little while feeling extremely embarrassed. Finally I asked if I could join the larger group. They were very friendly and welcoming. Everyone seemed amazed that I had been volunteering and they were all concerned that I was in a bungalow on my own. They even offered to escort me back, but I declined.

I loved being on safari, even rising at 4.30am for the 5am drive didn't bother me. We saw lions, leopards, elephants, giraffes... it was magical and I felt very privileged. The large group of tourists left after one day and I had the lodge almost to myself. I felt very grateful for the experience and returned home with wonderful memories.

• CHAPTER EIGHTEEN •

ITCHY FEET

In 2014 I decided to return to South Africa. I was keen to see more of the country, especially the lush "Garden Route", but escorted tours did not appeal to me, nor did the idea of hiring a car. After a bit of searching on the internet I discovered the answer: the Baz bus, "A hop-on, hop-off backpackers' shuttle service linking hostels". It sounded intriguing and I talked about it with my friends. They were all horrified. Rachel was my strongest critic: "You shouldn't do it, Jenny. You must be mad: South Africa is a dangerous place." Her words did not put me off although secretly I was a little concerned. I guessed that all the other passengers would be in their teens and twenties, while the word hostel conjured up visions of dormitories, shared showers and basic loos.

Three weeks before I was due to leave I had not even booked my first night's accommodation. Rachel was furious and I could see her point. Maybe I was too old for hostelling. I went home and googled "B and B's in Knysna". One called "Bamboo" caught my eye and I read some reviews: "Funky Knysna Guest House, the owners are very creative, we're talking recycling and inventiveness. The breakfast pancakes are the best!" wrote one guest. "Relaxed, friendly, quirky, artistic, tranquil, laid back, hospitable, homely, inspirational. Guests arrive as strangers and leave as family," wrote another. That decided me. I reached for the telephone and was connected almost immediately.

"Bamboo Guest House, Jaynie speaking."

The voice at the end of the line was so clear, it could have come from the next room. I took a deep breath.

"I'm a wrinkly English grandmother and I am going to be doing some volunteering in a township school near Port Elizabeth in January. But first I plan to travel down the Garden Route on the Baz bus."

Jaynie's response was immediate:

"Wow, you're brave! We'd love to have you staying with us. Our guest house is out of town but we travel in and out several times a day and we'd happily give you a lift." Her voice sounded warm and friendly.

"I'd love to come," I said.

"Great, tell us the time and we'll be at the Baz bus stop to meet you."

I put down the receiver feeling very relieved and reflecting on the kindness of complete strangers.

***

Four weeks later at 6.50am I was standing at the Baz bus stop in Port Elizabeth when the other passengers started to arrive. As I had predicted, they were young. Very young. Yawning and carrying massive rucksacks, they did not seem to notice me. My rucksack was tiny in comparison - I knew that I would not be able to lift a bigger one.

The bus drew up and as I looked at the high step I felt a momentary panic: would I be able to haul myself on? A strong sense of unreality struck me: was this really me? On a previous trip to South Africa Bob had been with me and we had hired a car. How my life had changed. Then I had felt safe and secure; now I felt terrified.

The bus passed through beautiful countryside but I was tired. I had travelled from England the previous day, stopping overnight at the Humewood Hotel to leave my case. I looked around at my fellow passengers. A young man opposite passed me a small book. "It's free," he said. Inside, all the hostels on the bus route were listed. I read it from cover to cover, the gypsy in me imagining staying at some of them. Many of the descriptions were very enticing. "Hands down one of the most beautiful places I have ever been to, beautiful vibes, beautiful people," said one reviewer, describing a hostel in Nature's Valley.

The journey from Port Elizabeth to Knysna took five hours, the bus stopping en route at several hostels. Just half an hour before we were due to arrive in Knysna, a girl got on and sat down beside me. We introduced ourselves: her name was Caroline, she was English, and she too was going to Knysna. By the time we arrived we had agreed to meet for supper that evening.

At last the bus stopped and I got off, relieved that I had negotiated the first part of my journey safely.

"You must be Jenny," said a young woman coming up to me, her hand outstretched. "I'm Jaynie. Come and meet my husband, Gordon."

Their car was very comfortable after the long, bumpy journey in the bus and Jaynie talked non-stop. "You're our first traveller from the Baz bus," she said, "you are very brave. We're amazed that you are going to be volunteering in a township."

"Are you hungry?" Gordon asked. I was: I had been far too excited and nervous to eat much on the journey. My hosts exchanged a few words then Gordon said, "Right Jenny, we'll go straight to a restaurant on Knysna Heads, you'll like it there." I murmured my thanks and 20 minutes later we drew up at a restaurant surrounded on three sides by the sea. The sun was blinding. The tables were laid with blue cloths and sparkling crystal glasses and for the second time that day I felt as if I was in a dream.

"I hope this is OK, Jenny. What would you like to drink?"

Jaynie's question brought me back to reality.

The wine arrived quickly, dry and cold. I wished that Rachel could have been there to see me. The meal was delicious and more wine was ordered as my new friends chattered, telling me about their lives.

Refreshed, we proceeded to Bamboo Lodge, where Jaynie seized my case and led me along winding paths to my room. First we walked through two doors set in a brick archway; they were painted turquoise and inset with lace panels. We entered a tiny courtyard and I saw a table and chairs and a sun umbrella. Plants climbed up the brick walls and there were flowers everywhere. I was entranced. My room was a feast of colour, with a woven tapestry on the wall and bright orange cushions on the bed. The en-suite bathroom was patterned in tiny mosaic tiles but by now I was too tired to take it all in. The combined effect of two days' travelling and the wine overcame me. I thanked Jaynie, lay down gratefully on the bed and fell into a deep sleep.

Several hours later I was woken by someone tapping on my door. It was Jaynie, come to take me to meet with Caroline.

Caroline and I ate a gorgeous meal and shared a bottle of wine. My new friend was blonde, attractive and in her late forties. In just two hours we learned a lot about each other. She was a divorced mother with a 19-year-old son. "This is my time now," she told me. "I plan to travel for a year and I may do some volunteering: I love animals. I'm going to find myself."

The wine was going down fast, Caroline drinking most of it as I was still trying to recover from the journey.

"I'm a widow," I replied, "I have one son and two daughters, two step-sons and eight grandchildren."

The bill came and Caroline and I agreed to share some of our time the next day together. I was astonished when she then ordered another bottle of wine.

"I can't possibly drink anymore," I protested, "I would fall asleep right here."

Caroline laughed. "No, it's for me. I'll take it back to my guesthouse. See you tomorrow."

***

I had planned to spend just one or two nights in Knysna but Bamboo was so special that I stayed for three. It was a fascinating place, quirky and fun, every corner holding a surprise.

"I love collecting things," Jaynie told me, and she displayed all her finds to great effect. There were treasures all over the garden: beautiful murals, mosaic birds, old garden tools colourfully painted, Buddhas and fountains. Jaynie's imagination, creativity and artistry permeated every corner and I spent hours exploring with my camera in my hand.

After a wonderful breakfast on an outdoor veranda listening to the birds singing, I could easily have stayed in the garden all day - but I had promised to meet Caroline to explore Knysna. We took a boat out to the Heads, climbed to the top and enjoyed the wonderful views. The scores of attractive gift shops which lined the streets were fascinating and at lunchtime, when we visited the local Rotary Club, we were made very welcome. There was just one black member and the average age was younger than my own club. The day was rounded off with a memorable walk in Knysna forest.

Caroline was fascinated by my description of Bamboo Lodge so I invited her back: I knew that Gordon was cooking a braii, a kind of barbecue, that evening. We joined lots of other guests, the wine flowed and the food was delicious. After two hours it was quite clear that Caroline was not fit to go back to her guesthouse. She had drunk far too much.

"Don't worry," said Jaynie, "she must stay with us."

I woke early the next day, breakfasted and swam in the pool. At about noon I met Caroline. She was very pale. "I'm going back to bed," she muttered and I never saw her again.

My next stop was Plettenberg Bay. I stayed in a clinically clean hostel that was almost on the beach. It lacked the charm of Bamboo so I only stayed for one night. It was exceptionally hot and I went into a sports shop to buy some sunglasses. I got talking to the sales lady and confessed my problems with the hostel. She told me that she had a friend who owned a guesthouse with a pool.

"It sounds lovely," I said.

A phone call and a few hours later, I was there. The neatly manicured lawns and hedges reminded me of England. The house was light and beautifully furnished. Josie the receptionist was kind and helpful, and we immediately became friends. I sat dipping my legs in the swimming pool, eating the sandwiches she had brought me. It was a welcome respite from my previous busy days and another example of wonderful South African hospitality. I spent most of the day in the pool, relaxing, later I went for a walk on a beautiful beach. Josie had kindly given me a lift.

"Are you sure you will be able to find your way back?" she said. I assured her that I would be fine. In reality however I spent one and a half hours trying to find my B and B. Every road looked identical to the last and I completely lost my sense of direction. In desperation I asked a man who was washing his car.

"You are miles out of your way," he said, "come on, jump in, I'll take you back."

In the evening I met other guests who were from Malawi. I quickly learned that they were Rotarians and we spent an interesting time comparing our two clubs.

In bed that night I read my little backpackers' book and decided that my next stop would be the "Wild Spirit" hostel in Nature's Valley. I learnt that it was a family-run hostel surrounded by indigenous forest, beaches and mountains. To quote from their website, "it is an experience in green living and alternative travel, catering for conscious explorers and open-minded travellers seeking something different off the tourist track."

When travelling across South Africa I constantly came across volunteering projects. Wild Spirit was no exception. It embodied the principles of permaculture, natural building and organic farming methods. It aimed to become a self-sustainable model farm and many volunteers came from all round the world. I talked with the owner of the hostel and learnt about the shot selling Fairtrade, free-range, local and seasonal products. I also learned of her involvement with the Bare Foot university programmes and her work with troubled teenagers.

Wild Spirit turned out to be a very good choice. The reception area was built of wood and a huge circular wooden sculpture flanked by driftwood immediately caught my attention. On the deck, tables were laid ready for the evening meal, and the views over forests and mountains were breath taking.

My room, which was decorated with pots and pebbles, was basic but comfortable and I could see for miles into the valley. Horses grazed peacefully in fields while back in the main communal area a cat lay sprawled on the table purring contentedly, several dogs laid stretched out on the sofas and chickens wandered amongst them. I walked over to the bar where a vase of sunflowers filled the room with sunshine. The volunteer helpers were called "Angels" and I was greeted with a smile as I ordered my meal.

I felt a little self-conscious amongst so many young people but the owner introduced me to Di, an American girl also travelling on her own. She was older than the other guests but much younger than me - she could have been my daughter. We got on very well and went out the next day to the Birds of Paradise Centre. The name rather put me off: I visualised birds in cages. However, I was pleasantly surprised. The cages were huge nets that reached high over the trees. The birds had so much space and it was fascinating to be able to observe them so closely.

The evenings at Wild Spirit were magical. As it grew dark on our second night, the fairy lights twinkled and an American singer, Brian Ernst, started to play. He had an incredible array of instruments - about 20 in all - including a hopping pedal. As the evening wore on he paused between songs and started talking about the charity that he and his wife, Katie, had founded. It was called "Journey for Youth" and they had started it in 2009.

As he quietly strummed his guitar, Brian told us about the backpacking trip that he and Katie had undertaken in 2010: they had lived and travelled in an old school bus that ran on waste vegetable oil. For the last three months of the trip they had lived with a family in a mud hut in Kaswanga Valley, Kenya. That experience had inspired them to start a daily lunch programme for 36 children, an initiative that ran from 2011-2014. Then they decided to change their approach, empowering people rather than giving them aid. They did this by granting micro-loans to small businesses.

I looked around the room as Brian played. It was dark, fairy lights were draped over the veranda and a huge log fire burned outside. Young hostellers sprawled on armchairs, others lay on the floor. A white lady, the owner, sat cuddling a small black baby in her arms. I bought one of Brian's CDs and I often play it - it brings back memories of a very special evening.

I wonder why our media focuses so much on the bad in the world rather than the good. Brian's passion shone through as he talked about Africa and how his experience there had changed him. He wrote a song, "Africa", as a call to his fellow countrymen to wake up and see beyond their affluent lifestyle. It was truly an inspiring evening and I felt eager to start volunteering again.

• CHAPTER NINETEEN •

STILL WANDERING

Memories of hostelling remained with me and on my last trip to South Africa I was eager to go further afield. I Googled "the Wild Coast, South Africa" and what I read enticed me: *"It is a place of steep green hills, a land of windswept cliffs, deserted white beaches, forest, and home to some of the most beautiful coastal scenery in the world."* I read further, my excitement mounting. *"The area is still somewhat lost in time – a place where hippies, surfers and Xhosa people live side-by-side with little in the way of possessions and much in the way of hospitality and friendliness."* I was a bit old to be a hippy or a surfer but I determined that I would go there.

Paul Miedema, the founder of Calabash, had told me quite a bit about Fairtrade Tourism South Africa in the course of our talks and I wanted to experience it for myself. I knew that Fairtrade tourism guarantees fair wages and working conditions, ethical business practices, respect for human rights, culture and the environment. I also discovered that there was a Fairtrade Tourism Pass that could be used in any Fairtrade tourism hostel. Curious to learn more, I sent off an email:

Help! I am a wrinkly English Grandmother. In February 2015 I will be volunteering for the third time at a township school near Port Elizabeth. I would like to travel on the Baz bus to the Wild Coast using Fairtrade accredited hostels. My friends think that I am mad.

A reply came back the next day:

Hi Jenny,

No you are not mad. You must come, you will love the Wild Coast. I will put together a wonderful holiday for you. Wait until your friends see the pictures!

***

In the weeks that led up to my departure the names of my destinations repeated themselves continually in my head: *Chintsa, Mdumbi, Bulungula.* By the time I came to leave England I was excited but nervous. Maybe I was too old to undertake a much longer journey on the Baz bus?

I set off once again on the now familiar flight to Port Elizabeth, staying overnight at the Humewood Hotel before going off on my travels. Sharing the Humewood with other volunteers was fine, but staying alone was not. There was only one couple in the dining room and six waiters hovered around me. The radio was, as usual, playing in the background and the music was interspersed with adverts imploring visitors to take out funeral plans. I missed my friends.

I woke at 5am and at 6.15am was once again standing at the Baz bus stop. It was exactly one year since I had last been there. I felt strangely free, unburdened by a case. The journey was beautiful and as before the bus was full of youngsters, all looking tired. Once again they took little notice of me. The driver told us he would be stopping en route at a small village. "The people are very poor," he said. "I always bring bread for them."

Half an hour later the bus drew to a halt. The street opposite was lined with people. I watched as the driver got off the bus with a huge basket containing loaves of bread. It was a small act of kindness, but one of many that I witnessed in South Africa.

As we drew nearer to Chintsa I remembered what I had read about it with increasing excitement: "A wilderness where man is part of the landscape not its un-ordained boss". I wondered what my hostel, "Buccaneers", would be like. Davina and Colin, my wonderful neighbours at home, had laughed as they had waved goodbye to me and wished me a good trip.

"Personally I prefer five-star hotels," Davina confided. I had laughed but secretly I was a little apprehensive.

My greeting at Buccaneers was warm. "You are our very first visitor travelling on the Fairtrade Travel Pass," the girl on the reception desk said, smiling.

My room was not ready so I went for a walk through the grounds and onto the wonderful beach below. A beautiful Labrador dog accompanied me as I wandered over planked pathways and wooden bridges. The sky was cloudless, the beach deserted.

Back at reception, Meg, the girl who had first greeted me, was waiting. "Jenny, please come with me. I hope you will be happy here." She led me down some steps to a bungalow overlooking the sea. "This is for you," she said, opening the door. I am sure I gasped in astonishment. A small, spotless kitchen led into a huge bedroom with floor-to-ceiling windows and a balcony with table, chairs and umbrella. The king-size bed had a white coverlet, huge squashy pillows and blue cushions; there were two couches and a large en-suite. It was perfect - how I wished that Davina and Colin could see me. But despite the wonderful setting I knew that I would probably have to spend the evening alone and I missed Bob desperately.

When I made my way back to the bar, I was glad to see Meg waiting for me. She beckoned me over and introduced me to the people sitting around her, people whose names I have sadly forgotten now. We all compared notes and I learned that one guy came from Kent where he lived in a village just two miles from Wateringbury: my home for 32 years. Meg put a large glass of cold white wine into my hand and I was made to feel very welcome, although everyone seemed surprised to see me. A chef from a nearby hotel introduced himself. "I'm J.C.," he said. "You're an inspiration travelling all this way alone." I think he was politely trying to tell me that I was very old to be undertaking such a journey.

"You must come for a meal at the hotel where I work," he continued. "You will be my guest; I will cook the best meal that you have ever tasted!"

I sat people watching and learned that all those around the bar apart from J.C. were employed by Buccaneers. Most of them were smoking and drinking heavily and someone thrust another glass of wine into my hand. The wine was strong and I was hungry and tired and anxious to eat. I rose eventually with as much dignity as I could and made my way to the dining room. The ground was very uneven and Meg, following me, shouted: "Mind the steps!" There were certainly a lot of them.

I was still concerned about sitting alone, but then Meg introduced me to Linda. "She is our school co-ordinator; she'll tell you about our volunteer programme." I was delighted and we spent an interesting evening together. Linda had an English degree from Canterbury University but had volunteered in Chintsa before starting at university. She couldn't forget the experience and had returned to work full-time for Volunteer Africa.

The next morning, I set off eagerly for Mdumbi. My little backpackers' guidebook had suggested that there I would: "Experience the culture, taste the lifestyle and breathe deep the rural peace of the Wild Coast. Enjoy the natural beauty of green hills and forests, secluded beaches, pristine rivers; you may never want to leave." Flowery words, but on my arrival at Mdumbi I saw that they were true.

It was getting dark and supper was being served when I arrived so I sat down immediately to a delicious meal of chunky vegetable curry, fish cakes and prawns. On my left-hand side was Jim and we talked throughout the meal. "I'm a failed opera singer," he told me. He had in fact been very successful, even taking some lead roles but then, "I lost my nerve. I was too frightened to go on the stage. I decided that I would travel; I don't think I can sing anymore."

Conversations in the hostels were generally much deeper than in normal circumstances. I met so many special people: a middle-aged American lawyer who was joining the Peace Force and proposing to work in Nepal; a young husband and wife who had worked on cruise ships and were taking a year out of their lives to travel; a Dutch dentist in his sixties whose wife had died, and Mike, who was running the hostel.

After supper Mike escorted me to my rondavel. It was very different to Chintsa, it contained a single bed and a shelf supported by driftwood. It was simple but I liked it and there was a small patio outside. My only worry was how I would get to the loo in the night. There were deep, rickety steps to negotiate and the path was very uneven so Dave lent me a torch. I had just settled down to sleep when I heard a noise on the patio. I tried to block it out, pretend it wasn't there but it didn't go away – thump, thump, thump.

My nighttime visitor

Eventually all was quiet and I managed to sleep but when I woke in the night I remembered it. Scared but needing the loo, I opened the door cautiously. There on the patio was a large dog. He yawned, stretched and got up, his tail wagging. I patted him and he rolled over on his back. I scratched his tummy and we became friends. He remained on my patio for the rest of my stay and I never felt frightened again.

In the morning the sun was shining as I made my way up to the main building. Breakfast was a casual affair; I ordered an omelette and sat looking out onto the most beautiful beach in South Africa with the waves breaking on the deserted sands. A rocking chair was strung invitingly between two trees. I moved to sit in it. In the distance I could see Xhosa women walking, carrying huge bundles on their heads, and hear children singing.

I didn't mind waiting for my breakfast, I was travelling slowly. Afterwards I walked, took photos and eventually wandered into the little nursery school just below my rondavel. The kids regarded me curiously, their eyes shining against their dark skin. In the afternoon I walked along the huge beach to the river, alone apart from one German girl. We met and talked for a few minutes. I learned that she too was volunteering.

Children from the nursery school

At supper I sat next to the retired Dutch dentist and two young South Africans who had travelled the world working on cruise ships.

On my second day at Mdumbi I went to meet the oldest lady in the village. She was probably about my age, but she had no birth certificate. Together with my guide I walked to her hut and found her sitting cross-legged on a bamboo mat. She beckoned me to sit down beside her but I declined, fearing I would not be able to get up again! The hut was bare apart from a stool and some cooking pots.

My guide translated and I asked questions, jotting answers in my small notebook. My new friend told me that men sit on one side of the hut and women on the other, sitting in line according to their age, and that large stones are used as pillows. I learned that women do the cooking; men do the gardening; their diet consists of rice, maize, beans, flour, coffee and powdered milk; illegitimacy is not accepted; marriages are arranged and people over the age of 53 get a pension.

When our meeting ended I offered the three-way Xhosa handshake and thanked my host. I reflected on how different our lives were. Supper that evening was a fish feast with salad – Israelis, Americans, Norwegians, Dutch and Germans sat at the table. At night there was a big party and I could hear the drums but went back to my room as I was tired. I missed Bob.

On my last morning I rose very early, just as dawn was breaking, and went for a walk along the deserted beach as the sun was rising. I had arranged for a kayaking trip at 7am: I had never kayaked before but I enjoyed learning the basics before gratefully relinquishing the paddle to my instructor. The river was beautiful: calm, peaceful and still cool. We saw four different types of kingfishers and some sea eagles. Plumbago grew in profusion along the banks reminding me of the design on my bedroom curtains. Forests of trees grew out of the water and poisonous jellyfish looked eerie yet beautiful in its depths. Returning to the hostel breakfast tasted especially good, and I was sad that I would have to leave Mdumbi in the early afternoon.

I travelled back to the main road with John, whose wife was a doctor at a hospital some three hours away. We had an interesting journey talking about the political scene in South Africa. John was a chartered accountant but was volunteering at the hospital doing manual jobs. I said goodbye at the local filling station. It was a busy place, the pick-up point for numerous shuttles like the one I was getting to Bulungula Backpackers Lodge (the journey there was far too difficult for the Baz bus). I was struck by the notice I read in the loo: "Be kind to those around you, human, animal or other. Honour the elements and the ground on which you walk."

Finally, the shuttle arrived and I squeezed in with six other backpackers. The journey was torturous - three hours on dirt tracks and pothole-ridden roads - but when I arrived I instantly knew that it had been worth it. Bulungula was magical! It was early evening, the sun was setting and the cluster of rondavels was suffused in a warm glow. Instantly, I felt at home. My new house was painted in a soft pink with a thatched roof and a stable door. Two horses grazed nearby and dogs and chickens roamed freely. Inside the hut there were just two beds. I laid my clothes on one and hung my towel on a stick suspended by two pieces of wood from the ceiling. On the walls were stylised trees painted in orange; outside I could see the ocean. I loved it!

My home at Bulungula

At supper I was joined by an American couple in their early sixties who were very complimentary about my exploits. "You must write for a magazine," the husband urged me, "what you are doing is very unusual." They were good company.

I was tired after my long journey and the showers were even further from my room than they had been at Mdumbi. They were the most extraordinary showers I had ever seen, decorated by a graffiti artist from London with brightly coloured animals. A trip to the loo, I thought, was like entering a modern art gallery or the illustrated pages of a child's book.

My guide showed me how to operate the shower: it looked incredibly complicated. "First put the paraffin into the small teapot here at the bottom of the shower, then light the wick with a match, like this." He smiled and demonstrated: there was a small bang and water trickled out of the showerhead. I thanked him, resolving to ask for more help in the morning when I would be less tired.

I slept well and woke early to walk on the beach before the sun was up. It was so beautiful: great stretches of golden sands and pounding breakers. Below my rondavel was a river flowing into the sea and cows grazed its banks. The beach was deserted. I turned right and walked along the coast, happily combing the sand for beautiful shells. After breakfast I explored my new home more. It was truly amazing; the paintings on the walls transported me to a wonderland of vibrant colour and quirky animals. Every surface was covered by curls, swirls and straight lines bisected by wonders from the deep. The mosaic flooring was lovingly created and there was colour everywhere: even the water tanks were painted in blue, orange, pink, green, purple...it was intoxicating.

The beach at Bulungula

The graffiti artist from London who had transformed Bulungula into a hostel of many colours was called Sarah Hubert, and I was lucky to meet her. I learnt that she had met Dave at a New Year's Eve party in 2003. "Back then, this place was just a dream in his head," she explained.

Dave had told Sarah about his ambition to build an eco-friendly hostel for travellers on the Wild Coast of South Africa and she had given him her address and promised to help if his plans became reality. In fact, she spent two and a half years at Bulungula, painting in schools, care centres and the project itself.

"Dave worked for a computer firm in London," Sarah continued, "he was highly skilled and very well paid. Finally, he had enough money to enable him to return to South Africa to find a location for his dream hostel."

Accompanied by a friend, Dave had walked for three weeks in remote areas, sometimes travelling by boat. Eventually he found Bulungula; with its beautiful beach and wide river, it was obviously perfect. Dave found a translator and found that the villagers were friendly and receptive - the hostel would mean paid employment. It took a year to obtain permission from the government and in just four months the lodge was ready. The building of it was a feat of courage, enterprise, imagination and huge physical effort. There was no electricity, no roads and none of the women had ever left the village. Dave told me of their incredulity when the first water gushed out of the tap. The hostel opened in 2004 and in 2014 Dave's dream was realised when he handed over the ownership to the local community.

Often in the dark, wet days of December 2015 I have re-read the description of Bulungula in my little coast-to-coast guide. I think it is worth quoting:

Overlooking ivory sands and backed by green hills that swoop down to sparkling sea, Bulungula offers intrepid travellers the opportunity to experience a slice of African paradise. The opportunity is also a challenge – to escape preconceptions and open your eyes, mind and soul. It's an invitation to experience a vibrant Xhosa community (who now own 100 per cent of the Lodge) on their own terms and to share their life. This jewel of a village, cut off from the outside world by forests, rivers and the ocean, was only accessible to 4x4s and intrepid hikers but now has a road accessible to all.

Unlike many travel brochures that exaggerate their claims, Bulungula was exactly as described.

By the time I arrived in 2015 the hostel and its programme was run entirely by the villagers. Dave had handed over responsibility but he was still there, keeping an eye on things. We had long conversations and he spoke passionately about Fairtrade tourism, but was fearful for its future and particularly worried about the financial implications.

"You have to pay to be Fairtrade tourism accredited, Jenny," he told me. "It is expensive and now the villagers own the lodge they may not be able to afford it."

Back in my simple room I had so much to think about. The Baz bus trip was opening my mind. I was seeing wonderful places and meeting inspiring people. Sarah had told me that she returned to Bulungula every January: she found it impossible to keep away and I could understand that. She had completed many projects, painting schools, hospitals and clinics, working with local people.

The incubator project

It was still only my first day at Bulungula and, deciding to explore further afield, I walked over the hills towards the village, passing goats, cows, sheep, chickens and horses. Finally, the sounds of children led me to a nursery school. It was completely different from any of the schools that I had seen in the township and I ventured in. Children were playing on a variety of apparatus: slides, swings, small scooters and climbing frames. Some were intent on building brightly coloured Lego. It was very impressive. I walked into an empty classroom where piles of books were neatly stacked, the walls covered in posters and children's work. The feeling was of an infant classroom in Britain.

The head teacher, whom I was fortunate to meet, was rightly proud of her school. She explained to me that it had benefited from the Bulungula "Incubator" charity. All the projects run by the community have been formalised into a separate non-profit making NGO. It had rehabilitated the local primary school, built and run four world-class pre-schools and two mini-clinics plus a number of ambitious agricultural projects, implemented clean drinking initiatives and lots more. Volunteers ran computer programmes at the primary school and extramural sports activities at another.

Whilst at the Incubator I met two German volunteer students who were working on an interactive maths computer programme. They were very enthusiastic and told me that they had used the working parts of second-hand laptops to make whole working laptop systems. Having begun in one primary school, they were now intending to roll out the programme to all the other schools in the area. I felt very inadequate! In this small rural village, almost cut off from the outside world, miracles were happening.

In addition to all this I learned that the Incubator project had won the McNulty Prize,[4] which is awarded to projects offering imaginative solutions to pressing problems that can be replicated elsewhere. Madeleine Albright was a member of the McNulty Prize jury and she commented that: "Many terrific projects approach a single issue across a broad field but Bulangula's mission is comprehensive. By finding a way to enact lasting change in this region, the Bulungula Incubator is a beacon for rural communities struggling with similar issues. Most importantly these communities have ownership over the improvements they make, creating a virtuous cycle of civic involvement and improvement in quality of life."

---

4 The John P McNulty Prize, which is worth $100,000, is given annually to honour the visionary work of a fellow of the Aspen Global Leadership Network.

I walked back to the village deep in thought. On one side of me was the lagoon, in front of me the sea. I had travelled so far and now in this beautiful remote part of South Africa I had found an amazing project.

Those four days at Bulungula will remain in my memory forever. It was responsible tourism at it very best, the food was gorgeous and a main meal cost just £3. At night I saw shooting stars and I still remember the evenings spent in a circle by the log fire, children from the village playing happily. Their numbers increased as soon as Herman arrived: he was a white South African in his sixties and a volunteer at Bulungula where he helped with carpentry and odd jobs. "I have never been happier," he said. "I play the drums and I am teaching the children. Stay around and you can hear them play."

Gradually more and more children arrived. They started banging their drums slowly, rhythmically, they were all very serious.

Every day at Bulungula was special. I combed the beach for more shells, took them back to my room and painted pictures of them. On the second day I went on a village tour with three others, a Zulu man married to a young Swiss doctor and her sister, a therapist. First we went to the home of the headman: it was very simple, just a large bed and a couch. I sat on the couch with four women, one the wife of the headman.

With the wife of the head man and her friend

Our guide told us that the headman was elected whereas the chief inherited his position and was in charge of several villages. The women chattered and gossiped, I guess it was the equivalent of a tea party! One lady wanted to buy my hair – she said I was very beautiful – and there was much laughter and incredulity when they learned that I was travelling alone. The guide translated: "They say you are lucky to be without a man, Jenny!" I did not think so. I missed Bob very much.

We left the house and walked on through the village to the sparsely-supplied shop. "When the owner runs out of stock, he closes the shop and goes off to buy more," our guide told us. We all sat in a circle, a bucket of beer was passed around and we were invited to drink. "Kneel on the floor and tip it up," our guide instructed, but I declined pleading age and aching knees. The shop was full and once again there was much interest and amazement that I was travelling alone without a husband. Many ladies commented that I definitely should not get another husband!

Our final visit that day was to the healer. We found her sitting cross-legged on a traditional bamboo mat, dressed in white and looking very sad. The women who were with her sat according to their age. We all shook hands.

The healer

"I never wanted to be a healer," she said, "but I was destined to become one. It was a gift from my ancestors. I had to learn to be a healer. I had to slaughter an animal and wear a band of fat and bone around my head."

I looked across at the young Swiss doctor: she was listening keenly and I reflected on the huge differences in the cultures of the two women.

"Do you treat people with AIDS?" the young Zulu asked.

"No I do not, I do not want anybody to say that I am a murderer. If my patients do not get better, it is because the ancestors do not want them to get better. I treat people with herbs, it is a way of speaking with my ancestors."

I longed to question her but felt it would be impolite. She showed us two sticks, one made out of plastic. "I keep these sticks beside me when I heal," she said. "My dreams enable me to know which of my children will become the next healer. If the spirits do not speak to my patients they must be transferred to hospital."

Finally we said goodbye, the two doctors had their photographs taken together and we went on our way. It was one of the strangest meetings of my life.

Bulungula was full of wonderful experiences and my third day was no exception. I joined Philiswa, a young single mother, for a glimpse of what it is like to be a woman living in the village. As we walked along she told me that she had a small daughter and a boyfriend. "He is saving to get enough money to marry me," she said. "When we marry I will live in his parents' house."

We set off together to her rondavel, friendly villagers waving and shouting greetings. One called out, "Don't take the old lady into the forest, don't make her cut wood." We visited a neighbour and I was glad that I could greet her in Xhosa. Finally, we arrived at a simply-furnished rondavel.

"I will make dinner," Philiswa said, "you can help me." She chopped cabbage and onions, added maize and put them all in a big pot to cook. "We will have this for lunch and supper tonight. Once a month we eat meat and we have porridge if we are hungry."

I looked around the room at the shiny saucepans. Philiswa saw me gazing at them. "They are for decoration only," she told me.

Dogs roamed in and out as we talked and Philiswa made a fire to cook the maize. "Now I will paint your face, Jenny, and then you will be a true Xhosa woman," she said.

I had already seen men and women walking around the village with their faces painted white: it was a form of protection from the sun. When Philiswa had finished with me she found a very old mirror; like my face it was small and cracked. I looked terrible.

The next task was to collect water from the nearest standpipe, a job traditionally done by women, who carry the water home in containers on their heads.

"Only the younger mamas do this," Philiswa told me. I felt she was being kind but I was thankful to be excused.

Back in the rondavel, after a simple but surprisingly delicious meal, we were joined by Philiswa's mum, auntie and toddler daughter. The little girl stared at me: she was truly beautiful.

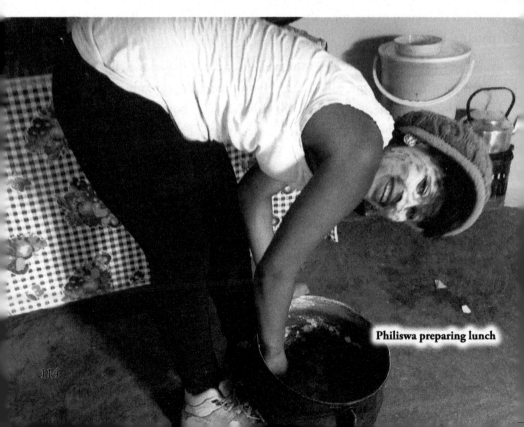

Philiswa preparing lunch

That last evening, I sat again around the campfire at Bulungula with the ocean below. One by one village boys and girls started to arrive and then the drumming began. One little boy, far smaller than the rest, was sitting on top of a roughly carved wooden seat. He paid no attention to the drumming and seemed lost in his own world. Suddenly he picked up a drum and began banging wildly. As he grew in confidence his drumming became rhythmical, but he played seriously and without a smile.

Herman came to sit beside me. "I am very proud of these kids,' he said. "I wouldn't want to live anywhere else in the world."

I got up early the next morning and walked along the beach for the last time. Dawn was breaking, the sands and the sea were vast. I was alone but for one fisherman sitting on a rock. I sat for a long time, willing myself to remember the moment.

Afterwards, I said my goodbyes: Sarah seemed sorry that I was going even though I had declined her invitation to smoke weed with her; Dave hugged me. "Do come back Jenny," he said as he took off his Fairtrade tourism t-shirt and gave it to me. "Make sure you wash it, it stinks," he laughed. I did wash it and it is still in my cupboard bringing back memories of a very special place.

And so I left, taking one last look at the small community that had taught me so much. Checko, the driver of the Baz bus, was exceptionally friendly and I felt like a seasoned backpacker as we drove away. I wished I was 20 again and at the start of my travels.

The final stop on my itinerary was Nelson Mandela's last home. It looked so different from the pictures I had seen on television after his death, when it had been thronged with crowds and media from all over the world. I gazed at the small brick bungalow attached to a larger building. The white South African government had given Mandela the house before the end of his prison sentence, but he had apparently chosen to live in the smaller bungalow. At that time the eyes of the world were on South Africa and criticism of the apartheid regime was at its height.

Many countries imposed sanctions and the South African government reacted by releasing Mandela from prison and providing him with this home. He was effectively free. The bungalow he had chosen to live in instead was small and simple and I felt very moved.

The Fairtrade Travel T-Shirt that Dave gave me.

I was happy to return to Chintsa and my lovely room with its balcony overlooking the sea. I spent my last day as a backpacker relaxing, walking along the sands and enjoying a massage. My trip to the Wild Coast had fulfilled all my expectations. When I finally returned to my home in the Lake District, Davina was there to meet me.

"The hostels were wonderful," I said, "even better than five-star hotels!"

CHAPTER TWENTY

WEEKENDS

At weekends we volunteers would often go for long walks along the sea front and always visiting the Sunday market in front of the Humewoood hotel. Spending hours looking at the wonderful range of handmade goods. It was a chance to relax, reflect and prepare for the coming week. Occasionally we would hire a car and visit another area.

One of our most memorable trips was to the Great Karoo, a vast semi-desert region with spectacular scenery. We managed to rent a house for one night, it had four bedrooms and a swimming pool and it cost us just £15 each. We arrived in the early afternoon and drove to the Valley of Desolation, it was eerily beautiful. We were fortunate to be there just before sunset. The huge pillars of rock called the Cathedral of the Mountains towered high above us, giant stone edifices three hundred million years old. The valley below stretched out for miles. I wandered away from the others and stood alone watching the sun go down, I felt very small.

The next day we drove to the town of New Bethesda where we visited Helen Martin's Owl House and Camel Yard. It was a strange, wonderful, inspiring and unsettling experience. I brought a small booklet and learned that Helen Martin was born in the town on 23rd December 1897 she had initially trained as a teacher, then briefly travelled with a theatre troupe, before marrying, divorcing and then returning to New Bethesda to look after her sick mother. Finally at the age of fifty she found herself alone in her childhood home. She set about recreating her own world,

eventually completing over 300 cement sculptures which still stand in her house and garden for everyone to see. I found it intensely moving, especially when I learned of her death by suicide. She made her home into a glass encrusted wonderland, using mirrors and glass to transform ordinary walls into glittering fields of colour. It was apparently called the Owl House because an owl had flown into the hospital ward where Helen lay dying.

Outside in the Camel Yard, so called because of the large numbers of life-sized camels, we wondered amongst the life-size statues. Some of the other volunteers hated it, but I was fascinated and could have remained there for hours. However other treasures awaited us.

We visited the fossil beds in the centre of town and looked at the 300-million-year-old remains of unique pre-mammalian structures in the rocks of the dry river bed.

Finally, we looked at the wonderful art galleries show-casing the work of talented residents. It was a truly memorable weekend.

CHAPTER TWENTY-ONE

SPECIAL MOMENTS IN THE SCHOOL

One morning I was in the staff-room marking. Cynthia was sitting beside me. A group of young people walked in carrying boxes, Cynthia hugged each one in turn. "They are ex-pupils of the school," Cynthia said, "they all work in the casino. Every month they save a percentage of their wages to help the little ones at Isaac Booi. They ask the teachers to nominate children who have worked hard and who do not have enough money to buy their own uniforms. We are going to have a ceremony. You can watch Jenny."

The young people unpacked the boxes, taking out new uniforms. Before long four little children marched in, standing tall and straight, they were about six years old. They shook hands solemnly and looked very proud as each of them was presented with a uniform. "Speech," cried Cynthia pointing to the children. She walked over to one of them, he looked very shy. "You must give a speech," she said, "you must say thank you for these wonderful new uniforms."

Looking at his feet the little boy mumbled something in Xhosa and everyone clapped. It was yet another example of the many good things that are happening in South Africa.

***

There were so many special moments during my three volunteering trips that it is hard to know which ones to single out, but the last morning of my 2014 visit is at the top of the list. Paul picked me up from the Hume-wood Hotel to drive me to the airport. I was wearing sunglasses; I did not want him to see the tears in my eyes. We drove through the affluent suburbs of Port Elizabeth; imposing houses, iron gates, spiked railings. I hardly saw them. In my mind I was back in the township, walking past the shacks built of corrugated iron and cardboard, past huge piles of rubbish and children playing in the dirt.

Paul interrupted my thoughts. "The school secretary has been phoning me all morning, asking 'When is Jenny leaving? What time does her plane fly?' I think some teachers plan to be at the airport. You have got under their skin Jenny; this has never happened before."

I was incredulous. "No Paul, you must be wrong, they will not be at the airport. I have already said my goodbyes. Today is a school day."

I thought back to the leaving ceremony the previous day: I had been more prepared than in 2013 and went to the staffroom already equipped with a box of tissues. As I stood there I heard drumming in the distance. "Come with me, Jenny," Cynthia said, "this is for you."

We walked out to the huge space between two buildings where assemblies were held. In front of me the school's majorettes team had assembled, ready to march. They looked amazing, their costumes having been donated by previous volunteers. The girls wore short maroon skirts, bright yellow jackets, huge white furry hats, white socks and white boots. The whole school had turned out to watch and when the music finally ended the little ones waved to me shouting, "Goodbye, Mrs Jenny."

This time I was prepared for the speeches and the singing but I was still very moved. These deeply religious people sang "We worship you, my Lord" over and over again. Cynthia swayed as she conducted the choir and Boni grabbed my hand. I was thrilled with the beautiful beaded necklace that I was given, a counterpart to the beaded belt that the school had given me in 2013.

Paul interrupted my reverie, "We're here Jenny," he said, he got out of the car and lifted my case onto a trolley. Then I saw them! Zozo, Cynthia, Ludwe, Miss January, Boni and many more.

"We have come, Jenny," Boni cried, "we have come to say goodbye."

There were tears, laughter, hugs, kisses, then Ludwe thrust a bundle of papers into my hands.

"We have brought you this, Jenny. It is the children's work."

I had marked it carefully, promising the kids that it would be displayed on the walls of the classroom. I could not hurt his feelings. I knew that somehow I would have to find room for it in my case.

"Why are you not in school?" I asked. "What about the children?"

"We have left them with the students, Jenny," said Cynthia. "This is important to me; come we must have a photo."

Farewell Jenny, at the airport

Boni unwrapped a huge South African flag and we stood in a line, passers-by gazing curiously. I smiled through my tears.

"Come on, Jenny, your plane will leave soon," said Paul.

At the barrier I turned and waved. I knew I was leaving a part of myself behind. Later, sitting alone as I waited to board the plane, I opened my iPad. I had asked Paul to take a picture of us all. I looked at those dear familiar faces and I saw that Boni's head was framed by a poster of Nelson Mandela. How apt, I thought!

CHAPTER TWENTY-TWO

REFLECTIONS

The teachers I met became my friends and as I got to know them better I realised that we had much in common. Like me they worried about their children, their jobs, their homes.

On my return from South Africa many people asked me if Apartheid still exists. Officially of course the answer is "no", but there is still a divide; the townships are separate from white communities and most of the children are educated in all black schools. In the shopping malls however there seemed to be no colour divide, as I have mentioned before, Zozo took me to one called Green Acres for a treat. It was glitzier and luxurious than many of the malls I have visited in Britain. She introduced me to her glamourous cousin who worked on the makeup counter. We walked in and out of the shops, Zozo brought a striking top and I spotted some lime green cushions perfect for my conservatory. Later as we sat drinking cappuccinos I reflected that not everyone from the townships could afford to visit the shopping Malls. "I am sending my kids to private schools," Zozo told me, "I want them to get a good education."

My first trip to South Africa with Bob was purely as a tourist. We had driven quickly past the townships, everyone warned us to lock our car doors. Through volunteering I gained a very different perspective. Zozo invited me to go and stay with her and her family. I would love to accept her invitation. We would often talk about our homes and one day we drove past hers, it was in the township and it looked very smart and well cared for. In 2013 two of the volunteers stayed at a guesthouse in the township and they invited us to visit them. From outside the simple bungalow looked modest but inside it was very luxurious; in the lounge there was plush furniture and rugs on the floor, chandeliers hung from the ceiling, the kitchen was a revelation full of gadgets and an American-style fridge. "Our guest house owner is a teacher," Sue told me, "she has worked for many years to make her home so special."

There were further surprises in the Township. Driving with Nelson one morning I spotted a white woman begging in the middle of the road by a set of traffic lights. I was astonished and Nelson even more so. "It is amazing to see a white woman begging," he said, "it is hard for me to believe, I was a child brought up in the Apartheid years, now I see white people facing difficult times. You will not see black people begging, they are very entrepreneurial; they will open small businesses." He told me that he had previously been at university pursuing a law degree, "I had to stop Jenny, I did not have enough money."

In the class room I was often amazed by the maturity and thoughtfulness of some of the older pupils. One component of the annual CAPS exams was an oral one. "Please will you help me test it," Cynthia had asked me. I can see myself in that classroom now as the kids prepared to give speeches persuading their classmates to elect them as councillors for their local area. I have a small video of the winner's speech as he stood proudly in front of the class, using his arms to accentuate what he was saying: "Thanks again for voting for me as your best councillor. I appreciate what you have done for me and I am going to organise some people to clean the classrooms and I will build book shelves. I will provide pencils and rubbers and all the stationary and every pupil will be important."

As I conclude this chapter I remember something else that Nelson told me in one of our conversations. "Many people have now left the townships Jenny, they have earnt a lot of money; their cars are worth more than their township homes, but they still return. Despite their wealth they love the close township community life."

When I look back over my photos and videos I see the poverty in the townships, but I also see the smiles and feel the hugs of the adults and children I was privileged to meet.

CHAPTER TWENTY-THREE

PAUL

I have alluded many times to the work of Paul Miedema and the Calabash Trust but before I end this book I want to write my own personal tribute to him. Sadly, he died at the age of 45 in February 2017. The success of our volunteering experience depended largely on Paul. Saga handled our initial enquiries, booked the Humewood Hotel and our flights, liaised with Calabash and sent us briefings, but it was Paul's support and leadership whilst we were in South Africa that was so vitally important.

On that very first day in Paul's office I can remember being impressed by his total commitment to the projects that he was supporting through the Calabash Trust. "You're not going to change the world in a month," he told us, "your volunteering will just be a thirty-day snapshot. I don't just see the snapshot but the whole continuing film about the positive impact on our Townships by you the volunteers."

He visited all the volunteers at least once a week, talking with the Principals and our teachers. Those weekly meetings were essential in the smooth running of our placements. We would gather in the staff room and everyone would have the opportunity to speak frankly. I remember telling Paul about the difficulties of being alone when my teachers were absent. Paul questioned me about what I did on those occasions and mildly rebuked me for not teaching from the syllabus. I reminded him that I had no syllabus and no books and that on this occasion the classroom door had been locked. I had been forced to think on my feet. The emergency lesson centred round my dog and my family. I think Paul got the point. I marvelled at his tenacity, enthusiasm and energy, for there were constant problems.

"I don't know how you cope Paul, how do you carry on day after day, year after year?" I asked him.

"I have to Jenny. I have no choice. What we are doing is so important." I agreed with him completely.

Thinking back on this conversation I feel deeply saddened by his loss, he is desperately missed, his vision and hard work enhanced the lives of hundreds of township people. More than five hundred gathered at a Thanksgiving service for his life. Thandi Miedema is now leading the work of Calabash tourism and the Calabash Trust, she and the staff are determined to carry on Paul's legacy.

Sallie Grayson from People and Places called Paul "a gladiator – a huge force for good – a passionate advocate for the people he worked with – an inspiration."

Many people have asked me if I would consider volunteering again and the answer must be "yes," although age and time are now against me. I would encourage anyone reading this book to volunteer. I gained far more than I gave, I learnt so much from Paul, my fellow volunteers and the men, women and children of the township.

CHAPTER TWENTY-FOUR

A BETTER WORLD

I am sitting in the conservatory of *Beckside*, my stone built Lake District house, on a beautiful June evening in 2017. The sun is setting on the mountains but my thoughts are of South Africa.

All around me are papers, scrappy notes in almost illegible handwriting: they are my book. It was not meant to be a book, when I first started writing it was just a paragraph. It is my first venture as a writer and I ask my readers to forgive any mistakes. It is a selfish venture, I need to put my memories down in print before they vanish, I am determined to preserve them.

My months in South Africa have taught me so much. I feel privileged to have shared teaching with Zozo, Cynthia and "Miss J" and to have become their friend. I remember all the staff, their exuberance, warmth, friendliness and strong religious beliefs.

"This is your school, Jenny, you are part of us," one of the teachers had said as I was preparing to leave for the last time.

"We will put your name on the door of a classroom, we will always remember you. We will say to a child, go to Mrs Jenny's room," another had said.

I had smiled to myself, thinking that they probably said the same thing to all the volunteers. Nevertheless, I was touched.

It was then that I was asked why I had returned to South Africa for a third time. I explained that I had read Trevor Huddleston's book Naught for Your Comfort when I was a teenager and the impact that it had had on me. I talked about the anti-apartheid marches and finally about how I had stood in Trafalgar Square to listen to Nelson Mandela when he came to England as President of South Africa.

Among the souvenirs that I brought back from my three volunteering trips, one is particularly special. It is a framed picture showing a phrase of Mandela's carefully stitched onto a canvas: "Education is the most powerful weapon which you can use to change the world."

Lightning Source UK Ltd.
Milton Keynes UK
UKOW06f1138100917

308802UK00006B/24/P